Starting a New Business?

Starting a New Business?

Think Big but Start Small

Chris Murphy

iUniverse, Inc.
New York Lincoln Shanghai

Starting a New Business?
Think Big but Start Small

Copyright © 2006 by Chris Murphy

iUniverse books may be ordered through booksellers or by contacting:

iUniverse
2021 Pine Lake Road, Suite 100
Lincoln, NE 68512
www.iuniverse.com
1-800-Authors (1-800-288-4677)

ISBN-13: 978-0-595-40037-9 (pbk)
ISBN-13: 978-0-595-84420-3 (ebk)
ISBN-10: 0-595-40037-X (pbk)
ISBN-10: 0-595-84420-0 (ebk)

Printed in the United States of America

Contents

Foreword

We are part of a global economy in which entrepreneurial opportunities are more evident than ever before as a result of upheavals in manufacturing, outsourcing and advances in communications and the internet. The way we start and run businesses has been drastically changed in just one generation. Entrepreneurs who are able to identify these opportunities and turn them into businesses will be the success stories of tomorrow.

The title of this book, "Think Big but Start Small," comes from years of experience in working with students and small business owners. The premise is quite simple: you do not have to spend a lot of money in getting your business started, let the business start itself. Several stories in the book illustrate this point. It is easier to get a business started today because a lot of the necessary information is quickly available on the internet. The previous generation of business people had to spend a great deal of time defining an opportunity and doing market research; at the library or through time consuming surveys. Today, both can be quickly accomplished using internet search engines. In 1980 you would have started a small shoe store on Main Street with inventory and a store front. Now you can sell shoes on line from your home office.

Prior to the availability of sophisticated business plan software, preparing a business plan was a dreaded chore and often did not include pertinent information. Now, there are several good software programs that make that chore much easier. One exceptional program allows you to customize your plan to fit the requirements of your business idea.

It almost seems to be a paradox that while the world is now your market and getting your business started is much easier, the basics still need to be addressed. You still have to research the opportunity and the market and create an operational system that will allow the business to grow. So, I have tried to link business start-up basics with the conveniences of modern technology. It is good to understand the basics even though technology has made it easier to get your business started. Each chapter addresses a different issue in the start-up process, first with the basics, then with the technical resources available to you. An example is in Appendix A, in which the web addresses of over two hundred business resources are listed.

There are a lot of books available on the subject of starting your own business and some of the better ones are written for a specific type business such as "How to Start a Landscaping Business, or How to Start a Ceramic Business." They are helpful because they deal with the specific steps required to start that type of business, and are generally written by someone who has been successful. Entrepreneur Magazine offers a number of these "How To" manuals. Other start-up books are written from a particular viewpoint. For example, if the author is a former CPA, you can count on a full accounting and data management treatment. One author I know is a former SBA official and his approach to starting a business is a rather rigid set of business plan guidelines and a procedure leading to an SBA loan. There are also the generalists who write business books with lengthy explanations of minute things that you may never use in your business. These authors are generally business school professors and professional writers who have never been in business. As a friend of mine says:" If you want to learn to play golf take lessons from a professional who has lots of experience, not from someone who has read lots of books on the subject but never played the game."

My approach to the subject comes from 35 years of starting, operating and subsequently selling a variety of 16 businesses. I have experience in retail, wholesale, franchising, manufacturing and banking. I have received numerous Entrepreneurship awards and have taught a variety of university entrepreneurship courses. I believe this experience is reflected in the following pages.

Introduction

America is in the midst of a revolution! Entrepreneurship has never before been as dynamic or made such an impact on our economy as has in the last decade. It is estimated that five of every ten working Americans have thought about starting a business of their own, and that three of these actually take the step to business ownership. The result of this surge of business owners is that 60% of our gross national product and 70% of employment is from the small business sector. This is unprecedented in our history! According to the SBA about 2 million new businesses from one-person shops to multi-million dollar enterprises will be launched this year alone (1). And for every start-up that fails nine new ones will begin. About all newly created jobs come from these and expanding firms, not from the large corporations. The result is that employment in small firms is growing three times faster than employment in the 500 largest companies according to a study done by American Express (2).

Despite what you may hear, half of these start-ups will NOT fail in five years. Tim Hatten, a Colorado State University Professor of Entrepreneurship, says: "this is a myth that will not die." (3) Even the Advocacy Office of the SBA reports that when mergers, name changes, incorporations, closing to retire and other non-financial reasons are considered, failure due to bankruptcy is only about 6%. Why are these statistics important? because, I do not want you to start with a fear of failure. Instead, if you follow the concepts outlined in this book you will consider yourself so well prepared that you are confident of success. Planning is the key. If your plan is complete, confidence is increased and risk is minimized.

An interesting phenomenon has developed in the high-tech arena as a result of small business companies competing with the large corporations. In an environment where technology, competition and the desires of the marketplace change quickly, a small business is more flexible and can take advantage of changing conditions. The big corporations with chains of command and levels of bureaucracy are slower to move so their size and capital advantage is eliminated when they compete with the new, more flexible and faster moving companies. The best examples are found in the hi-tech industry where new high-tech and "dot-com" companies have swept the landscape with innovative businesses that have left the big corporations in a position of being customers and not originators.

This entrepreneurial wave will continue for many years into the future and the opportunities for people who are innovative and know the basics of getting a business started will be on a continuing upward curve. Teaching entrepreneurship has grown from a hip pocket, trial and error practice to a science with over forty scholarly journals devoted to the subject. There are stories of musical prodigies who never had a lesson but could play the piano beautifully, just as there are stories about successful business people who never took a course in entrepreneurship. There will always be these rare exceptions in any discipline or effort, and for every one of these exceptional people there are thousands who have tried and failed. I am convinced that had some of those who failed been given proper instruction in how to develop their idea into an opportunity; how to assemble the necessary resources and how to create a plan for their business, they would have been successful. The purpose of this book is to provide some of that guidance and to give those who want to start a business of their own in this new high-tech economy the tools they will need to be successful.

Chapter One

Getting Started in Entrepreneurship

> *".....and let us not weary in well doing for in due season we shall reap if we faint not." Galatians 6:9*

There is no mystery to starting a business; it is a fairly straight forward process that simply requires planning, good judgment and some background in the business you want to start. But, as the above quote suggests, it is not easy and it takes perseverance. It is much like building a house. First, you start with an idea, then a set of plans. You build the house one board at a time until it is complete and you are ready to move in. In the process you may need the help of a carpenter, plumber, electrician or mason because you can't be expected to know everything. The same is true in starting a business. You will need the help of some experts like a banker, attorney, and an accountant. This course will put all these things in perspective to help you avoid making a costly mistake along the way.

The fact that you are reading these words suggests that you are thinking about starting a business, and you want to find out all you can about how to get it started and be successful. The information in the manual is based on my own experience in starting businesses and on the experiences of many people I know who have successfully started and operated businesses from start-up to sale of the business. There is a common denominator that creates a path to success in business that if studied and practiced can greatly enhance your chances for success.

Can anyone start and run a business? The quick answer is no. Just as there are a lot of people who cannot learn to play the piano. Of those who try, some will be happy doing well with chopsticks, while others will only be satisfied with Mozart. In the second chapter I will cover some of the personal attributes necessary to start and manage a business. There is a lot of research on this subject and we know there are people whose personal traits do not fit the requirements of business ownership. It is a good idea to find out right away if starting a business is for you. Some of the unhappiest people I know are those who invested their life savings

1

in a business they now hate, but are trapped and cannot get out. Understanding that successful business ownership is not an easy journey and that there will be challenges and detours along the way is half the battle. The other half is being sure that your personality traits are the right fit for business ownership.

There are many books available on Starting Your Own Business. You may have found this out by now. It is confusing to decide which of the 40 selections in the library you should choose, or which of the ten to twenty current titles at the local book store would be best. I recommend that you select one that is pertinent to the type of business you plan to start. As a rule of thumb, the books with the catchy and cute titles generally lack substance, and the really good books tend to be too academic; concentrating on details or discussing ventures that require over two million dollars to start. I will stick to the basics with this thought: *"Think big, but start small."* There is a third part to this mantra and it is *"Think Smart,"* which involves careful planning and using current technology to your advantage.

Think Big, Think Smart and Start Small

One of the biggest mistakes people make in starting a business is not giving themselves enough credit. This is partly due to the fear that they might fail and will lose the time and money they have invested. It also results from a serious lack of planning before they open the doors. Planning is the key. If a good road map of where you are going and how you will get there is prepared, then the possibility of failure is greatly diminished.

The basis of this road map is "Think Big, Think Smart and Start Small." Attending to the last part of this mantra is *don't invest more than you can afford to lose.* The planning process should tell you where you will start to make money. In other words, your cash flow should support your business at a certain point in time, and it is important that you know how many months it will take to reach that point.

Let's go back to the "Think Big" part of this equation. Many start-ups limit their view of the future with rationalizations: "I just want a comfortable business that I can enjoy," or, "I don't want it so big that I can't handle it." Or the worst: "I just want to see if it has the potential to grow." The new business owner should know the growth potential of the business, this is part of planning. In cases where businesses grow in spite of the owners they may find themselves working 70 or 80 hours a week, with no time of their own. The business controls them; they do not control the business. Patricia Cloherty, a well known venture capitalist says: "It is critical to think big enough. If you want to start and build a business, you are going to wind up exhausted anyway, so you might as well think about creating a big business, at least you will end up exhausted and rich, not just exhausted (4)."

How does a person wanting to start a small business get the odds of success in his or her favor? Analyze the industry you are in; check out trade associations, go to the internet and find the SIC code for your business. Do some research through the Robert Morris Associates (RMA) to find out the success and failure rate of similar businesses. You can bet your banker will if you apply for a loan. Bankers know that 61% of business failures are in the retail and service sector, the highest being in the restaurant business. Overall, the failure the failure rate for start-ups is 46.4% in five years. Real estate with 36.8% is the lowest. These figures are published by the Small Business Administration and I will discuss them again late on. The success and failure ratios for your business are very important to your planning. You improve the odds by knowing what the chances for success are in your industry.

Another factor that causes smaller businesses to fail is that they tend to be job substitutes and are undercapitalized, under managed and often poorly located. According to the *Bizminer 2002 Startup Business Index* (5), the one year survival rate for businesses with 1 to 24 employees is 53.6%, while the success rate for companies with 50 employees is 69%. This tells us that the larger the business the greater the chances for success.

So, while it is smart to start small in order to test the market and get your feet on the ground, set your sights high. Plan on 15% to 20% growth every year, and know what you have to do to accomplish this growth. Set goals of where your sales will be at the end of each year, and what your cash flow will be. Go out to the fifth year in your planning and if your business has not tripled in size you need to find out why.

What in the World is Going On?

As previously mentioned, in any given year there will be over 2 million new business start-ups in the United States, and this includes every conceivable type of business from a corner hot dog stand to a bank. This represents about 1% of all working adults. The SBA Advocacy Office says that about half of this group will think about starting a business at some time in their careers. Something like 40% will investigate what they see as an opportunity. About 10% actually do something like buy a book or attend a seminar, 5% will take direct action and become discouraged by the challenges, and it is the final 1% who start planning and subsequently open a business.

According to the SBA, the impact of small business on the U.S. economy is profound. Here are more statistics (6):

- There are 28.5 million small businesses in the United States.
- These businesses represent 97 percent of all employer firms.
- They employ half of all private sector employees.

- They pay 44.5 percent of the total U.S. payroll.
- They generate 60 to 80 percent of all new jobs annually.
- They create 60 percent of the GDP (Gross Domestic Product).
- They employ 40 percent of all high tech workers.
- They make up 97 percent of all identified exporters

Many of us start businesses a few years after graduating from college, partly because we know the effort we are giving an employer can be applied to our own business. The mark of a true entrepreneur is an inability to work for someone else. Progressive educators recognize the economic importance of this surge in entrepreneurship. Research shows that two thirds of all college students intend to be entrepreneurs at some point in their careers and yet business school textbooks stress large rather than small firm examples. They have also found that people with more education are more likely to become entrepreneurs. Classrooms, both within and beyond schools of business, are filled with potential innovators. The key is to provide the necessary skills that will allow them to foster these talents and start new businesses.

In the early 1970s only 66 colleges and universities offered courses in entrepreneurship. Today there are almost 1800 two and four year colleges and universities offering these courses. In addition, several states have passes legislation that will require the teaching of entrepreneurship in grades K through 12 (7). Entrepreneur Centers have sprung up in the more progressive universities where business school educators and entrepreneurs get together to exchange ideas and to draft educational programs to meet the challenge of the new entrepreneurial economy. Unfortunately, there are still many business schools that do not see entrepreneurship as a viable curriculum and will continue to prepare students to "find good jobs" teaching them to become "obedient employees." In one respect this provides a balance because those who are creating new businesses will have a source for employees.

We All have the Potential

According to Jim and Joanne Carland, Professors of Entrepreneurship at Western Carolina University, people starting businesses have different capacities, or potential for success (8). They designed the Carland Entrepreneurial Index, an assessment of potential ranging from mom and pop stores to a Bill Gates type mega corporation. They found that we all fall somewhere in between. Simply stated, some of us are happier with a flower shop than we would be with a multi million dollar high tech business.

Start-up businesses tend to fall into one of four major categories:

1. **Have something to do.** In most cases these people have another source of income; retirement, pension or a great severance package. Generally, they are over 45, they have energy, active minds, ambition and are anxious to maintain a daily routine. They want the flexibility of having their own business, choosing where it will be, when they will work and what kind of business they will have. They are often a husband and wife team and mutually agree on the type of business they want. The profitability of the business may be secondary to their purpose. If it breaks even they are happy. Many of them use the business as a legitimate reason to write off vacations as business trips and to take them as business losses against their outside income. It is also not unusual for people in this category to turn a hobby into a business, or to simply pursue some activity they have had in mind for a long time. There are many franchise programs that attract these people because they can step into a business with very little training and with promises that franchisors know they want to hear. The term, "Mom and Pop" business generally applies to these people. The typical business plan intended to attract financing does not apply to them. However, a modified strategic plan that will serve as a business road map is necessary.

2. **Make a comfortable living.** People in this category are tired of working for someone else and they want to see a financial return for their own time and effort. Typically, they have thought about the business they want for a long time and have accomplished some degree of market research and a lot of planning. In many cases the idea for the business developed as a result of something they were doing on the job or a need they see in the marketplace. The reason they have not started their business is either financial or the fear of losing the security of working for someone else. The allure of "having a business of my own," gets stronger as they see others going into business, possibly with very business idea they have been planning. Sometimes this occurs with a patentable idea. They often succumb to the dictates of the heart and try to start a business without adequate planning in order to be first. The failure rate of those who let their heart rule is very high. On the other hand there are others in this group who will take the time to construct a good business plan and will go into business with a solid foundation of information, data and financial planning. They plan to start their new business on a small scale, within the constraints of their financial ability. These people will succeed and it is this group to which this book will appeal.

3. **Get rich quick.** It is difficult to understand but there are still some people who believe they can get rich in multi-level marketing programs, pyramid scams, stock and option schemes and chain letters. These people are not looking for a business but for a one time hit. They read the back pages of business pulp magazines or see testimonial advertisements on TV by shysters to

claim you can make thousands of dollars in a short period of time with very little investment of time or money. They sign on to multi-level merchandise scams with promises of getting rich simply by recruiting others who then recruit others. The advertisements that promise these things should be against the law for it is false advertising. This book does not subscribe to, or promote, any get rich quick scheme. Instead, people who are considering one of these schemes are urged to read this book and to begin developing an opportunity for themselves in a real business.

4. **High stakes ventures.** One of the most interesting developments in our new economy has been the emergence of multi-million dollar ventures and the willingness of investors to back them financially. These ventures have a very high success rate and investors hope there will be a good return on their money. Ventures in this category follow the curve of economic interest and for the last decade that interest has been in sophisticated technology. However other business areas that have innovative concepts have also attracted investors. Here, more than in other innovative businesses, the extent to which there is excellence in planning and a strong management team, will determine the interest of venture capitalists. Taking an innovative idea and turning it into a business opportunity that will attract investors is a task that requires a well-written business plan and previous experience. It also requires the ability to articulate the concept and its requirements in a way that is knowledgeable and convincing. If these factors are present, and the financing to get the business started exceeds one million dollars; the chances for success are very high (9). The reason for this correlation is easy to understand. Investors will make sure that the plan is sound and that the management team is capable before backing the venture. Smaller business ventures can learn from this by putting the same ingredients into their proposals before presenting their plans to banks, family or friends.

Needless to say, most of us are in number 2, "Business as a Life Style." And it is to this group the following pages are directed. As I have stated: the more you plan, the greater your chances for success. Or, as the old saying goes: "The harder you work the luckier you get.". Chapter One covers the dynamics of entrepreneurship. Chapter Two looks at the personal traits and characteristics. Chapter Three talks about passion and innovation. Chapter Four discusses the type of business that is right for you. Then, Chapters Five through Nine go into the mechanics of putting your business together, and finally Chapter Ten goes through the business plan process. As an added feature, Chapter Eleven gives you a step by step process for starting a business in the five main categories: retail, wholesale, service, manufacturing and E-commerce. All of the essential elements of getting your business off to a good start are explained in a way that is easy to understand.

Chapter Two

Do You Have What it Takes?

> *"You just keep pushing. You just keep pushing. I made every mistake that could be made, but I just kept pushing"*
>
> Rene McPherson

The easiest thing to say is that you are the only one who has the answer to this question, but research has shown that there are ways to measure your potential for success. You may be highly motivated and have a great sales ability, but this does not mean you can handle the trials and challenges of business ownership. Quitting a full time job to start a business is a giant step and you should assess the proposition carefully before making the commitment.

How far along are you in thinking about the business you want to start, and what have you done so far? You may have had an idea for a business for some time now and need to know the next step. Or, you may feel you are ready to open the doors and are simply looking for some guidance. In either case, the same basic rules apply and this course will help you to achieve your goals.

Let's get started with this short questionnaire; truthfully answer yes or no.

1. I have a good idea for the kind of business I want to start.
2. I think I have the aptitudes and personal skills to run my own business.
3. I have put some money aside to start my business.
4. I know that starting a business will not be easy.
5. I have discussed my business idea with family and friends.
6. I have a good idea of the market for my product or service.
7. I am willing to put 100% of my time into my new business.
8. I am tired of not being paid for my time, ideas and energy.

Hopefully, you answered "Yes" to all of these questions, because each one represents an important party of the business equation. A "No" answer may suggest that you need to go back and rethink that subject because this course will depend on your commitment in each of these areas. For those of you who want to start a business but do not know what kind of business, there are some suggestions at the end of this section.

As previously mentioned there are three reasons businesses fail: lack of planning, poor management, and running out of money. I will add two more reasons: lack of experience in the type of business you want to start and the personal inability to cope with the rigors of business ownership. While these may be considered a part of management, they stand out as handicaps to success in business ownership. One reason people start a business is because they have have experience in that field, and feel they can either do it better or simply see some of their employer's weaknesses as an opportunity.

Your Strengths and Weaknesses

You will seldom find a person who has all the qualities needed to be successful in business. Everyone has strong suits and weak points, and the same is true of business owners. It is necessary to understand those strengths and weaknesses. To do this, you need to evaluate the major achievements in your personal and work life and the skills you needed to accomplish them. In the same manner be honest about your weaknesses. For example do you hate selling? How about cold calling a prospect? Keep in mind that selling yourself to a customer is the most important key to your business success. Are there other things you dislike doing that will affect your business? Don't be afraid to make a list of both your strengths and your weaknesses. Begin to plan on how you will improve in those weak areas. For example, if you hate speaking or selling then you can join Toastmasters or take a Dale Carnegie course and that will help tremendously. Or, maybe you feel a weakness in bookkeeping. There are excellent short courses in bookkeeping available.

What are Your Goals?

In addition to evaluating your strengths and weaknesses, it is important to define your business goals. Is your goal the freedom to do what you want when you want to without anyone telling you otherwise? Or, is it simply financial security?

Setting goals is an important part of the planning process, and as we shall learn later on they are also an important part of your written business plan. Think about it, if your business does not meet your personal goals, you probably won't be happy getting up every morning and trying to make the business a success. When setting your goals use the following guideline:

1. **Be specific:** "I want the chance to earn more money," is not specific. "I want to have a net profit of $10,000. by the end of the year is specific.

2. **Be optimistic:** "I hope to be able to pay my bills'" is not up-beat. "I will achieve financial security," is optimistic.

3. **Be real:** Do not set goals that are unattainable. Remember the adage we will repeat several times in this course: "Start small, think smart, plan big." In thinking smart you will tend to underestimate and not overstate.

4. **Short term and long term:** In the short term, what can you actually accomplish in the next eight weeks, or the next six months? These are things you know you can do because your research says you can. In the long term you will state what you *hope to do* and probably what your trade association predicts you can do.

Probably the most important thing in setting goals is honesty. Going into business with your eyes wide open about your strengths and weaknesses, your likes and dislikes and your ultimate goals lets you confront the decisions you will face with greater confidence and more assured success. One of the objectives of this section is to give you an opportunity to analyze your motives for starting a business, your personal attributes and your objectives. The best way to do this is for you to complete work sheets designed for that purpose on the next few pages.

Personal Goals and Objectives Questionnaire.

Setting goals not only gives you an ongoing road map for success, but it shows you the best alternatives should you need a change along the way. You should review your goals on a regular basis. Many business people do this daily as it helps them assess their progress and gives them the ability to make faster and more informed decisions. Fill out the following questionnaire. At this point in your planning process you will find this very helpful in setting and resetting your goals.

1. The most important reason for being in business for myself is:

2. What I like best about being in business is:

3.   Within five years I would like my business to be:

4.   When I look back over the past five years of my career I feel:

5.   My personal financial condition as of today is:

6.   I feel the first thing I must do to start my business is:

7.   The most important part of my business is (or will be):

8.   The area of my business in which I really excel is:

Once you have completed the Personal Goals Worksheet, put it aside as we will be come back to it later. It is quite possible that after you have studied other parts of this course you will have a different perspective than you now have.

This next worksheet was originally developed by Northwestern Mutual Life Insurance Co. with their permission. It is widely used by schools, counselors and agencies of the SBA in helping people take a look at their personal attributes as related to business ownership. It is by no means a scientific assessment and is used here only as a way of looking at some of the personal qualities considered important in business. There are other validated assessments available if you are interested in a scientific appraisal of your personal traits as related to entrepreneurship. Check out www.biztest.com.

What is Your Entrepreneurial Quotient?

Common characteristics in areas such as family background, childhood experiences, core values, personalities and other factors turn up time and time again in studies of entrepreneurs. Find out how you fit the mold by determining your Entrepreneurial Quotient, or EQ.

The following questionnaire is not a measure of your future success as a business person, but it may show where you excel and where you need to improve to help make your business a success. Answer the following questions with a "Yes" or "No" and total your score at the end to find your EQ.

1. Did your parents have their own business? _____
2. Were you a top student in school?_____
3. Did you enjoy participating in group activities in school, such as clubs. Team sports or double dates? _____
4. Did you prefer to be alone as a youngster? _____
5. Did you run for office at school or initiate small businesses at an early age, such as lemonade stands, newspaper routes, or cookie sales? _____
6. Were you a stubborn child? _____
7. Were you a cautious youngster? _____
8. Were you daring or adventurous? _____
9. Do the opinions of others matter a lot to you? _____
10. Would changing your daily routine be an important motivator for starting your own business? _____
11. You might really enjoy work, but do you object to working through the night? _____
12. Are you willing to work as long as it takes with little or no sleep to finish a job? _____
13. When you complete a project successfully, do you immediately start another? _____
14. Are you willing to commit your savings to start a business? _____
15. Would you also be willing to borrow from others? _____
16. If your business should fail, would you immediately work on starting another? _____
17. Or, would you immediately start looking for a job with a regular pay check? _____
18. Do you believe that becoming an entrepreneur is risky? _____

19. Have you put your long and short term goals in writing? _____
20. Do you believe you have the ability to deal with cash flow in a professional manner? _____
21. Are you easily bored? _____
22. Are you an optimist? _____

Scoring the Entrepreneurial Quotient

Each question in the EQ questionnaire is scored individually as follows, starting with the first question: <u>Keep a running total of your score.</u>

1. <u>If you answered yes, score one point. If no, subtract one.</u> *Significantly high numbers of entrepreneurs are children of parents who owned their own businesses.*
2. <u>If yes, subtract four points; if no, add four.</u> *Successful entrepreneurs are not, as a rule, top achievers in school.*
3. <u>If yes, subtract one point; if no, add one.</u> *Entrepreneurs are not especially enthusiastic about participating in group activities in school.*
4. <u>If yes, add one point; if no, subtract one.</u> *Studies of entrepreneurs show that, as youngsters, they often prefer to be alone.*
5. <u>If yes, add two points; if no subtract two.</u> *Enterprise usually can be traced to an early age.*
6. <u>If yes, add one point; if no subtract one.</u> *Stubbornness as a child seems to translate into determination to do things your own way, a trait of successful entrepreneurs.*
7. <u>If yes, subtract four points; if no, add four.</u> *Caution may involve an unwillingness to take risks, a handicap for someone embarking on uncharted territory.*
8. <u>If yes, add four points.</u>
9. <u>If yes, subtract one point; if no add one.</u> *Entrepreneurs often have the faith to pursue different paths despite the opinions of others.*
10. <u>If yes, add two points; if no subtract two.</u> *Being tired of a daily routine will often become the reason for an entrepreneur's decision to start a new business.*
11. <u>If yes, add two; if no, subtract six.</u>
12. <u>If yes, add four points.</u>
13. <u>If yes, add two points; if no, subtract two.</u> *Entrepreneurs generally enjoy their type of work so much they move from one project to another–nonstop.*
14. <u>If yes, add two points; if no, subtract two.</u> *Successful entrepreneurs are willing to use their savings to finance a project.*
15. <u>If yes, add two points; if no, subtract two.</u>
16. <u>If yes, add two points; if no, subtract four.</u>

17. <u>If yes, subtract one point</u>
18. <u>If yes, subtract two points; if no, add two.</u>
19. <u>If yes, add one point; if no, subtract one.</u> *Many entrepreneurs make a habit of putting their goals in writing.*
20. <u>If yes, add two points; if no, subtract two.</u> *Handling cash flow can be critical to entrepreneurial success. Learning how financial statements work in your business is very important.*
21. <u>If yes, add two points; if no, subtract two.</u> *Entrepreneurial personalities seem to be easily bored.*
22. <u>If yes, add two points; if no, subtract two.</u> *Optimism can fuel the drive to press for success in uncharted waters.*

Determining your EQ.

Total your score.

A score of 35 or more. You have everything going for you. You have the potential to achieve the success you are looking for.

A score of 15 to 34. Your background skills and talents give you excellent chances for success.

A score of zero to 14. You have a head start of ability and experience in running a business and should be successful in opening an enterprise of your own if you apply yourself and learn the skills to make it happen.

A score of–1 to–15. You might be able to make a go of it if you start a business, but you will have to work extra hard to compensate for a lack of built-in advantages and skills that give other entrepreneurs a leg up in starting a business.

A score of–16 to–43. Your talents probably lie elsewhere. You should consider whether building your own business is what you really want to do because you may find yourself swimming against the tide. Working for a company, developing a career, or achieving an area of technical expertise may be far more appropriate to your abilities and interests.

Again, these last two questionnaires are not scientific appraisals of your potential to succeed in a business of your own, but are included here to give you an opportunity to begin thinking about your personal qualifications to run a business. It isn't for everyone and the saddest person in the world is one who runs a business he or she hates. It looked good from the outside looking in, but once the realization that it takes total dedication, those who are not cut out for self-dependency begin to suffer.

Based on what we have just learned, let's take a look at some of the personal skills you will need to run a business:

Be Success Driven: This business is your baby and you need to do everything possible to make sure it grows properly, prospers, and makes a profit for you. How badly do you want to win? What are you prepared to do to get there? It is very likely that you will invest heavily in your business to meet early requirements, so you may have a lot to lose if it fails. In addition to tapping out your personal finances, doing everything possible can mean driving 400 miles in one day to bid on a contract that is important to you. Look back at your career; have there been times when you gave up easily when a hard challenge faced you? Or, did you get steely-eyed and resolve that even if you are pushed beyond your limits you will succeed in solving a problem? I have found that some new business owners, who were unenthusiastic when working for someone else, will break out with tremendous energy and ideas when it involves their own business.

Running a business can be stressful. The pressure and excitement can sap your energy and strength. If you do not have the energy required it may be difficult to get up early every day, even if you love what you do. You need to know that you are in good physical health. Keep in mind that the health insurance you depended

on while working for some one else will probably not be there in case you get sick. True, there is COBRA through which you can continue your former health insurance for a period of time, but it will run out. Health insurance is expensive as you may have discovered. If you have any preexisting condition that may develop into hospital time, you may want to re-think your decision to go into business at this time.

Multi-Tasking: From the first day you open the door on your new business you will find that nothing is predictable. Every day will offer a different set of challenges, problems and decisions. To many business people this is part of the excitement in owning a business. How many times have you been bored in your job because you knew exactly what you would be doing the next day? You need to be flexible enough to change strategy at times and stick to your plan at other times. It is a question of balance and you should expect to make mistakes while you try to find a solution.

Self-Reliance: This is probably the most important of the Personal Characteristics. The old saying: "The buck stops here," is certainly true when you own your business. In working for a company you had others to rely on for various things, and they depended on you. In your business you are the only one. You are a salesperson, an operations manager, a delivery person, a human resources manager, and by the way, you are also the president of your company. You must make decisions. You cannot hesitate and pray for a miracle; you simply make the decision and accept the consequences. Being the one who is ultimately responsible for the success or failure of your business means you have to train yourself to take action when necessary and not merely react. You can teach yourself to do this. Always maintain a sense of urgency. If there is a problem, solve it now. If there is a decision to be made, make it now. If there is a job to be done don't put it off until tomorrow.

Self-Discipline: Owning a business is an exercise in self-discipline. In the early years of starting a business such things as vacations and free week-ends are generally replaced by getting things done to meet the requirements of the business. The demands of the business will take precedence over many of the things you took for granted when you were employed. You may have guilt feelings about wanting to devote yourself to your new business, after all it's your baby and it needs care. However, for the sake of sanity you will need to allow some time for leisure activities so you will need to strive for balance in your work and home life. The key to balance is time management and your commitment and discipline to follow a schedule.

Commit to Goals: Setting periodic goals is one way to sustain your drive, and committing to accomplishing each goal can be the fuel that sustains your drive. The goals should be realistic and attainable. We discussed how to set goals early in this chapter. They should be set up on a monthly basis to begin with then on six month intervals after you start your business. Establishing goals will be the backbone of your business plan, and each goal will be supported by facts and figures. We will discuss how you put it all together in the last session. Just be aware that you need to determine what you want to accomplish, how you will do it and in what period of time.

There are probably other personal skills dictated by the nature of a particular business, but for our purposes here those I have listed above will be necessary for any business owner to be successful.

There will be Risks:

One of the things we tend to take for granted while employed by a big corporation are such things as health insurance, vacations, maybe a car and an expense account, and a regular paycheck. When you start your business these things might end. For example, one of the risks you will encounter is the loss of guarantees you may have enjoyed as an employee. It is also a rule of business ownership that chaos will prevail because you will be making all of the decisions and taking on all of the responsibility. Murphy's Law may be the order of the day, "*Things go wrong at the worst possible time.*" I can add that Murphy was an optimist.

In the first two years of building your business you should not plan on vacations, week-ends off or a regular pay check. Your time belongs to your business, and if you are reaching your goals perhaps your financial projections will predict when you can draw a pay check from the business.

In essence, you are gambling with your life, time and money, and it would not be at all unusual at this point if you were a bit unsure about the decision to start a business, knowing how it will affect your family, life style and your own well being. It is important to be aware of the risks before you take the big step. It is also important to know that it is through this rite of passage that you can achieve a better life that you ever thought possible

Money IS the Issue.

Money is the reason you are starting a business and you need to know how to make it work for you. Remember: *Don't spend more than you can afford to lose and don't lose what you have.* Later on when we discuss the importance of a business plan we will go into the financial aspects of your business. For now, I want you to concentrate on two things: how are you going to maintain your personal finances while starting your business, and how are you going to raise the initial money to get it started? Unless you are an exception to the rule you will not be able to pay yourself a salary for several months so it is important that you identify this phase of your planning as critical. If you have a large inheritance or have won the lottery you can skip this session, otherwise read on. If you have set realistic goals in your business plan you know when your business will start to show a profit. It is that period of time from when you first open your doors to when the business begins to make money we are concerned about. If your husband or wife can continue to work and supply the household income until that time–great, if you have saved enough money to sustain your household that is good too. I suggest that you prepare for this period of time by establishing a household budget–even if you have not had one in a long time. Streamline your personal financial situation as much as possible. You may want to consider meeting with a CPA to explain your plans and have her help you set up a personal budget and a start-up budget for your business. Do these things before you quit your present job. One more thing, banks are not a resource at this point. They will want to see a complete business plan and they will not loan you money to start your business unless you have adequate collateral and the ability to make a personal investment in the business.

How is Your Credit?

This is a good time to ask the question that banks, vendors and anyone else supplying you with things that involve credit will ask: Is your personal credit in good shape? At some point in the process of getting your business started this question will come up, but instead of asking you directly the lender or supplier will simply check your credit score through one of the three credit reporting agencies. If your score is low you will not get a bank loan and you will have a very difficult time getting credit from suppliers. So what do you do? You can request a copy of your credit report for a small fee (usually about $8.50) or free in some cases. If you have been turned down for credit because of a low score then the information must be supplied to you at no cost. Requests should be made by calling one or all of the following. Or, access their web sites for an overview of their services.

> **Equifax**, P.O.Box 74024, Atlanta, GA, 30374. Phone 1-800-685-1111
> **Experian**, P.O. Box 949, Allen, TX 75013. Phone 1-888-397-3742
> **Trans-Union**, P.O.Box 390, Springfield, PA 19064 Phone 1-800-493-2392

If you have been denied credit, the Equal Credit Opportunity Act requires creditors to tell you the reason you were rejected, (if you ask), for 60 days after being denied. If you have poor credit do not be dismayed. Credit records can be improved by contacting those who turned you in and finding out why they did. There are many mistakes made in the credit reporting business, and it may be that your score is the result of faulty reporting. You need to take the action now to get your credit in shape if there are some problems. Of course, paying bills on time and paying down outstanding balances always helps.

Family and Friends.

It is quite possible that both family and friends will think you have lost your sanity because you want to change course at this point in your life and start your own business. First of all, they do not want you to upset the status quo and they tend to judge your action as a loss of security.

Another interesting fact that researchers have discovered is that your family and friends could be jealous because they know you might become successful. Many entrepreneurs use these things as fuel to fire their ambition to prove they can do it. But, family and friends can also become an ally in getting your business started. Once you have shown them your business plan and they can see your resolve in starting your business they can become your biggest supporters, both financially and morally.

Time is of the Essence.

One of the biggest risks in starting a business is that you will simply run out of time to get things done. Time is the most precious resource you have. If you started a business against the advice of your friends and family who think you are crazy anyway for quitting a good job, then you are particularly aware of the ticking clock. The advice of many business owners who have experienced the same restraints of time is: "Don't cut corners on service or quality to meet a deadline. Don't say yes to every project or customer who comes to your door. Take the time to do it right and do only what you are capable of doing." Keeping your perspective is essential to running a growing and healthy business.

Time management is essential, especially if your business requires you to adhere to deadlines. Train yourself to allow more time to complete a job than you would normally take. This goes against a business owner's natural tendencies and has to be incorporated first in your thinking and then into a daily routine. Prior to this someone else may have structured your time for you and set deadlines. Now it's up to you and it may not be easy. Again, it is important that you adopt a sense of urgency in everything you do and that you maintain this feeling once your business starts.

Wealth Opportunity:

The monetary rewards from being successful can be great. But it is not unusual for a successful business person to say that it is the *sense of accomplishment* that outweighs the financial benefits they reaped. Once you have become successful and are accepted as part of the business community people will come to you for advice. Just as you should seek counsel from business people who are successful in your area of interest. It may have taken you five hard years to become an "overnight success" but you have survived the ordeal of the start-up years and you are now an expert in their eyes. When your business is going great and you have hired people to do many of the things you had to do in the beginning, you can concentrate on the second phase of your business career, that of growing and expanding your business.

Your Business Idea:

People start businesses based on a hobby they enjoy like furniture refinishing, antiques or flower arranging. Others will see an opportunity based on their current job; something they can do better, or an area their employer does not want to pursue. I know of cases where an employer has financed a business for a former employee knowing it will save them money by outsourcing to someone who understands their needs. Still others will start a business because they saw one in another city they liked and feel it will be successful where they live. Typically, entrepreneurs see that a problem can be solved with new product or service, then research the market to determine the extent of the need, finally they develop the product. There are many reasons people identify with a particular business and feel it will be good for them, needless to say a lot of investigation and planning will need to precede start-ups of this kind. Hopefully that is why you have this book in your hands right now.

Then there are those who want a business but have not decided on the business that will best for them. They are either retired or simply tired of working for the other guy and are looking for the right business. There are two ways to begin your analysis of possibilities: *Franchising*–which we will discuss at length in chapter five, and *Opportunity Recognition*–which I will discuss now.

What kind of business should I start?

There are opportunities all around us, many of which we take for granted, and others that we simply overlook because we are not aware that it is an opportunity. Entrepreneurship is the act of finding a profitable solution to a problem. Every successful entrepreneur is someone who has been able to identify a problem and discover that the solution to the problem is a business opportunity. Here are some examples of going from problem to idea to opportunity as proposed by Brian Tracy in his *Five Rules for Business Startups*. (10)

1. **Find a need and fill it.** When Ross Perot was working for IBM, he saw that his customers, who were buying IBM computers, needed help in processing their data. He went to IBM with his idea, and they were not interested, so he started his own business. He eventually sold Electronic Data Systems, Inc. to General Motors for $2.8 Billion. He found a need and filled it.
2. **Find a problem and solve it.** A secretary working for a small company began mixing flour with finger nail varnish in order to white out the mistakes she was making in her typing. Soon, her friends were asking if she could make some for them and she began mixing it on her kitchen table. The requests grew and she eventually quit her job and began started a business called Liquid Paper. A few years ago she sold her company to Gillette Corp. for $47 Million.

3. **Look for solutions.** Find a way to supply a product or service better, cheaper, faster and easier. Clemmons Wilson saw that there was a need for hotels that could accommodate families that were traveling, and he started Holiday Inns. Now one of the most successful hotel chains in the world.

4. **Focus on your customer.** Become obsessed with your customer; fixated on his needs. What does he want and when does he want it? How much does he want to spend and what his problems are? Tom Watson, built IBM on this principle. See yourself as working for your customer.

5. **Invest sweat equity in your business.** Most great fortunes in America were started with an idea, personal effort and with the sale of outstanding services. This is called sweat equity. In other words, instead of cash equity, put in sweat equity. Once you have come up with a product or an idea, start to invest your time, talent and energy instead of your money to get it started. Many businesses start small and with great effort develop a cash flow that finances their growth. A former student of mine started a trash collection business as a class project. He began by offering to pick up trash from each apartment in his building. His concept was good because he knew people did not like to take their trash to the dumpster outside. He charged them $15.00 per month and signed up all twelve units in his apartment building. He had $180.00 in positive cash flow. He then signed up all of the units in his complex, and by the time the class semester was over he had $900.00 per month in gross sales. He hired two students part time to help him paying them $2.00 per bag, amounting to $120.00, so he had $780.00 monthly profit. This was sweat equity; he never had to borrow money to make money.

What do you do?

First, find a need and fill it. Look around you and search for needs that people have for products or services that are not being met. Like my student, one small idea is enough to get you started. It is often a good idea to spend some time in a large city to see what is going on that is not being done where you live. I often recommend that one week in Los Angeles will give you lots of ideas. Everything seems to start in California.

Second, find a problem and solve it. Look around you for problems that you or your friends have that are not being solved. Then, look for solutions that nobody has thought of and give it a try. Another student of mine noticed that people had problems keeping grocery carts from rolling in the parking lot, so he invented a simple brake that operated on the push bar of the cart. The solution to a problem does not have to be highly technical. Matter of fact, the simpler the better. One good solution could change the direction of your life.

Third, become an avid reader of business publications. I recommend INC magazine, Entrepreneur magazine, and any of the other business oriented publications that you will find in the local book store. In addition, the Monday edition of the Wall Street Journal, the local Business Journal and any other local business magazines. All of these sources let you know what is going on in your area; the businesses that are getting started and even the money the SBA is approving for business loans. If you are going to become a business person it is important that you start reading business publications.

Read this short case about a new business that just opened and see how you would have handled the situation.

The Ned Jones Incident

Ned Jones had just opened the doors of his new franchise muffler shop. He had completed three weeks of intensive training in management and operations at the franchise headquarters, and had carefully ordered his inventory according to a study of vehicle demographics in his area. He was bursting with energy about his opening day and as proud as a new father would be of a first child. Everything had gone according to plan; the advertising was in place, his new crew was well trained, the equipment was installed and ready and Ned was waiting for the first customer, which would be sort of special. Into the lot drove an old 1976 Buick that looked as if it should be in a museum. Ned's crew put the Buick on the lift and looked at the exhaust system. It all needed to be replaced. Parts of it were suspended by wire coat hangers. Ned did not have a single part for it in stock. He explained to the elderly owner that he would have to special order parts for it and that it might be next Wednesday before they would arrive. With that the customer said "You are guilty of false advertising because your ad says you can install a muffler on any car in 20 minutes, what's this about?" Ned replied, " Sir, first of all your car is 27 years old and I don't even have a listing on it in my parts catalog, but its also important for you to know that it needs more than just a muffler. It needs a whole new exhaust system. This will take about two hours to install when we get the parts." The customer replied, "All I need is a damn muffler and not a lot of lip from you. You people are all alike, ready to take advantage of an old man. Just forget it and get my car down, and I'll tell you right now that I plan to report you to the Better Business Bureau for false advertising."

In your answer try to show how this negative situation can be turned into something positive and how Ned can create a customer instead of losing one.

Also remember that someone who creates a problem generally has a problem to begin with..

This brings us to the close of our first chapter. Hopefully you have learned that there are some personal characteristics unique to successful entrepreneurs and that most of them can be learned with diligence and personal introspection. You have also learned a little more about what it takes to run a business and at this point you should have an idea of where you may need some help.

Anyone can start a business but not everyone can be successful. Thorough planning is the key. Inadequate planning is the primary reason for all of the business failures. Part of the planning process is making sure that the business you want to start is the right business for you. The quickest way to run a business into the ground is to start the wrong kind of business. That is what we will discuss in the next session,

---

Chapter Two Summary Quiz

1. What personal characteristics should a business person possess, and why are they important?
2. Why is it necessary to "like to deal with people" in order to be successful in business?
3. What are the risks in starting a business?
4. What are the rewards?
5. Why are both a personal and start-up budget necessary in the beginning?
6. Why is a "sense of urgency" important?
7. Why do family and friends have to be carefully considered in the start-up process?
8. Why is it important to have a good credit rating when starting a business?
9. List the reasons why time is so important in the start-up process.
10. Why is it important to set goals at this time?
11. What should I do If I don't know what kind of business to start?

Chapter Assignment:

What are your goals? Go back to pages 8-9 and follow the directions for setting your business goals.

Chapter Three

Innovation and Passion the Key Ingredients of Success

> *"Imagination is more important than knowledge."*
> Albert Einstein

This chapter is for those of you who do not know what kind of business to start. You have the desire and motivation, but the opportunity; the right business, has not presented itself.

According to Webster innovation is the act of introducing new things or methods. Ray Kroc was innovative when he created the McDonalds way of selling hamburgers and Colonel Sanders did it with Kentucky Fried Chicken. Certainly, hamburgers and fried chicken were not new but these men were entrepreneurs. They knew the old saying, "It ain't the steak that sells, it is the sizzle." It was the innovative way they merchandised these foods that made them so successful. Home Depot, Lowes, Walmart and Office Depot do not offer anything that was not offered before by the small neighborhood stores, but these giants saw the needs and buying habits of an expanding and changing urban America and answered with innovative and dynamic merchandising techniques. The small neighborhood stores are gone and some people may argue if this is good. The answer is that we are a dynamic society whose buying habits are constantly changing and it is the successful entrepreneur who can feel the pulse of the buying public and respond to it with new ideas.

There are people who share the opinion that the way to success in business is to select a successful role model and emulate them. Certainly you would not try to copy Walmart or Home Depot. First, it would be too expensive, and second, you would not be successful if you did because they have captured those markets. More importantly, if you try to copy a successful business you can duplicate the obvious techniques that they practice, *but you cannot capture the passion that drives their success.*

Passion follows innovation. In many cases passion is a result of the criticism and the negative judgment of others that results when an innovative idea is presented. Therefore, passion is a result of the conviction that your idea is right and that it will work. Every great business idea is met with criticism and negative judgment from those who do not share the passion. It is almost as if this is the necessary rite of passage or process that a new idea must go through to harden it into an opportunity.

It is an interesting phenomenon that when someone announces to family and friends that he or she is thinking of starting a business, the first response is almost always negative. Generally, the most negative reaction is from family, who you would expect to be the most supportive. Then friends, who will one by one tell horror stories of people they knew who failed in business. One can only speculate at the reason for this negative judgment, but it is reasonable to assume that it is honestly because they are interested in the welfare of the person proposing the venture. Family and friends do not want you to venture into a possible failure. More specifically, they do not want you to change the basic patterns of your life or theirs. Picture this scene: You are enjoying a backyard cookout with family and friends on a beautiful Saturday evening. You decide this would be a good time to announce your plans to quit your job and start a business of your own. You do not plan to go into all the details of the countless hours you have spent planning and researching your business idea or how recent changes in the product market you are planning have opened the window of opportunity for you. Your plan to use this occasion to tell them about starting your business because you want them to share in your joy and possibly because you have found financing for your business. Your spouse is aware of all these things but is fearful of the "unknown." Your friends will give you tacit support but warn you of "all those dangers." This reaction is so common that it has aptly been labeled, "The Voice of Judgment." The one thing you want most will not be there, and that is unqualified belief in your judgment and wholehearted support. It is speculated that the reason for this is because friends want to keep things as they are. There is a comfort level that has been established and they do not want to have it upset. Family, on the other hand, does not want to see the nest disturbed. You have a good job with security and a retirement plan. Why would you jeopardize all this just to satisfy your ego and start a business of your own? Isn't that being selfish? If you are convinced that your idea will work then you are passionate about it and then "Voices of Judgment" will only strengthen your commitment.

Instead of negative judgment, please support me:

1. Listen to what I have to say and try to understand me.
2. Even if you disagree with me do not try to prove me wrong.
3. Accept my passion for this idea and look for the greatness.
4. Tell me the truth, but with compassion.

It generally takes time and patience to satisfy these questions and it is the start of the gauntlet you will go through. The process of answering the doubts of everyone in your life sets you apart. And, this solo role is one that you will play on a full time basis as a small business owner. You will not have the comfort of going to someone in the next office for advice because you are the problem maker and the problem solver. It is a lonely role and the challenges of growth, finance, management, and human relations need to be as exciting to you as the business idea itself.

Developing the Idea.

It is important to understand that innovation is important to the success of your business. As pointed out in the beginning of this chapter, you may attain low to moderate success by imitating the techniques of a similar business, but you will never attain great success. Assuming that you are starting a business to make money, then it follows that the greater your success the more money you will make. So, how do you insert innovation into your business idea? Let's take a pizza business as an example. There are a lot of them so it will be easy to do. You will want it to be different from all the others because being just like the one down the street and advertising the same way will not attract customers. When one pizza parlor advertises a $5.99 Special, you can bet their competition down the street will answer with a similar ad. This is letting competition determine pricing, which is also wrong. In developing your marketing strategy you will first study the strong and weak points of every pizza parlor in your area. The franchised programs will be at the top of your list because they have spent millions of dollars to show how they are different and why their pizzas are better. So you will carefully study each franchise, taste their pizzas and document the outstanding features of each one. Having diligently compiled this information you will then devote a good deal of time in research to summarize the strong points and the weak points of each one. Then you will have an expert look at your summary to get an objective opinion. From this you will determine what innovative strategy you can develop and what you will have to do to make your pizza parlor different. It is from that point that you will begin determining your plan of action. *You are selling the difference, not the pizza.*

While this is a simple example, it represents the basic steps you will employ for any business idea. Innovation and creativity must be a continuing part of your business, not just the beginning. So you must adopt a different way of looking at the obvious things around you to determine a new way of doing them. Being able to do this will set you apart from your competition and put you in the position of trendsetter and innovator. This concept is more difficult than envisioning an innovation in the pizza business because you first have to get out of the unseen box in which you are living and view your surroundings from a different perspective.

We are Pre-programmed.

It is an interesting fact that from the time you could talk you have been programmed to get a job. When small you were asked, "What do you want to be when you grow up." Many of us thought being a policeman an airplane pilot or a nurse would be nice. Then in high school and college it became serious. You were taught a trade, aimed toward a profession, or taught how to write a resume. It is unlikely that anywhere along this route you were given instruction in how to open your own business. It is even more unlikely that you took an entrepreneurship course in school. Fortunately that is changing in many schools today. But it remains that 99% of adults have had no instruction or early incentive to start a business. You are expected to be an employee not an employer and this conditioning is one side of the box.

Social expectations, peer pressure and pre-conceived ideas make up the rest of the box. You live, work and do things in certain predictable ways that are expected. Break away from what is called the "norm" and teachers, friends, employers and family call you to task. Your life is charted and you are expected to stay on the course. You are taught to look at things a certain way and to accept them as fact. In order to look *outside* of the box you need to understand that you have been preconditioned, and understand the reasons why. Great business innovators, and certainly the inventors who hold many patents are people who see beyond the walls of the box and who chart their own course. They simply see things around them differently than others. It is important for you to understand this concept and to begin developing the innovative skills that will be critical to the success of your business.

Try the following two exercises as a test of your **observational skills** and the first step in critical analysis:

1. Carry a note pad and pen with you for at least seven days. Jot down everything that either aggravates you or something you would change. Make these simple things like

the location of a stoplight or the way you are treated in a restaurant, not big things like the failures of government or a foreign country's bad attitude. The man who became aggravated at the one speed windshield wiper on his car sat down and invented the variable speed motor that is used on all cars today. First, you will find that the act of writing these things down is not easy to do simply because it is not part of your usual routine. Do not pressure yourself. The first day you may only have five or six items listed, but then as time progresses you will find it easier to do and perhaps fun. Then your list will grow. You may even want to continue the process for several more days. This accomplishes several things: First, it forces you to see simple, uncomplicated things differently. Then the act of writing them down causes you to analyze what you have seen or experienced. You have never done this before and you are taking a critical view of things that everyone else is taking for granted, therefore you are thinking outside of the box. At the end of the seven (or more) days go back over your list and this time write down what you would do to change those things you have observed. The significance of this exercise is that you have begun the process of critical observation, which is the first step in developing innovative skills.

2   This next exercise in innovative thinking will also require one week, and the hardest part of it demands *no television!* When you get bored with the exercise you can read, take a walk, jog or just talk to someone. You have a choice; if you have no artistic ability then you will paint a picture. (Do one painting and schedule your time for one week). Or, build a model airplane. The idea is for you to commit to a task that you would normally not choose to do, so if neither of these apply to you select a task for which you feel you have no aptitude or ability. Spend the week devoted to completing the task. Program your time and make sure you have the materials to complete the job. At the end of the week ask yourself these questions and write down your answers for future reference:

> A.   What did I learn about myself?
> B.   What was the reaction of others, and what questions did they ask?
> C.   What problems did I encounter in completing the task?
> D.   Was I critical of myself (voice of judgment) or encouraging?
> E.   Did I complete the task and was I proud or disappointed?

By doing something totally foreign, and within certain time constraints in the absence of distraction, (TV), you are again looking outside of the box. People who have done this exercise generally learn that given an opportunity to accomplish a task on their own, where they set their own time schedules, they succeed. The feeling is one of accomplishment and the greatest distraction is from others who question your intent and purpose. You may experience a sense of purpose and pride (passion) as a result.

It will be the same when you start your business. You are responsible for your schedules, time commitment and the setting of goals. If things do not get done you alone are responsible. Is this a challenge or a something you hate? It is better to find this out now rather than waiting until after you have opened your business. You need to feel passionate about every aspect of your business. Did you ever notice the look on the face of basketball players in the final game of a major tournament? You see the passion to win; the ability and the determination to successfully accomplish a task within the constraints of time and rules. This is the same passion you need to be successful in your business. Learn this now. Adopt passionate attitude about your business and all the challenges that go with it before you make an investment of time and money.

Are you listening?

In the mid 1960s the Radio Corporation of America (RCA) developed a management training program called "Developmental Counseling." It was designed to help managers counsel their employees in a constructive way by teaching them *how to listen.* This program was developed because it was recognized that managers could not counsel their employees if they did not know how to listen. There is an old saying: "We have two ears and one mouth therefore we should listen twice as much as we talk." Just as RCA found, if their managers learned to pay attention in the form of listening, they became better managers. If this same ability is put on a national scale, just learning how to listen could affect the American economy and psyche. (I do not mean cell phones).

For lack of listening, billions of dollars of losses accumulate: retyped letters, rescheduled appointments, and rerouted shipments, breakdowns in organizational communication, misunderstood sales presentations and meaningless employee performance reviews. Certainly, in starting a business the ability to listen is critical to the process of developing an innovative strategy. In doing market research, contacting prospective vendors, negotiating with landlords, interviewing employee applicants and surveying potential customers, critical listening skills are required.

Many businesses find the quality of listening important enough to emphasize it in their advertising. It is not uncommon to see slogans like: "We understand how important it is to listen." "I'm probably the best listener you will ever hear," and "What's the point of talking? You don't listen anyway." A 1985 *Fortune* article carries the title: "How to Sell by Listening."

What is true listening? Check a dictionary and you will find a real difference between "hearing" and "listening." The definition for hearing is "the capacity for auditory sensations." The definition for listening is "to pay attention, to give heed, to apply oneself to hearing something." So hearing is the capacity to receive the sounds, while listening is the act of paying attention to the sounds themselves. Most of the sounds you hear are words. By developing these words into phrases, then into sentences, then into paragraphs, you do something called communicating. Questions and answers, statements and responses. What could be simpler? But, do you listen to what is being said as well as what is being unsaid? People communicate with words as well as body language. How does bias or emotion affect what is being said? We all come from different backgrounds; so many times certain words have different meanings. It is only by careful listening, paying attention, asking questions and recognizing that there are barriers to the communication process that can keep understanding from taking place.

Good listening is the basis of innovation and creativity in your business. Management expert, Tom Peters, with his idea of "managing by walking around," and Rene McPerson, with his emphasis on "managing from the bottom up," base their approaches on true listening. When Peters' managers walk around, they listen to what people are saying. McPherson describes his own open-ear management this way:

"Oh, that's easy. Start before everybody. Work harder than everybody. And just use all the people assets. There are hundreds of them all around you. All kinds of people surrounding you who are willing to help you, and nobody ever asks them. And you go ask them for help, and you work with them, and they just love you to death, because you came and asked them "What do you think?" and you are genuine about it." (11)

Communication is often blocked because of preconceived opinions. How often have you made up your mind before the person to whom you are talking has finished? How often are you influenced by how that person looks? During a meeting with several people, or listening to a speaker, how often have you so concentrated on what you want to say or ask that you have not heard what is being said? These are listening habits that block understanding and are not constructive. Being aware of your own listening habits is the first step to learning how to communicate in a way that leads to understanding and to innovative action.

Putting it all together.

Innovation—*offering something in your business that no one in similar businesses offers*-is going to be the key to your success. The process of determining what that "something" is will require strategy, planning and perhaps an attitude change on your part. Listening to your customers, advisors, vendors and competitors will give you the *creative difference* you will need.

Forget about it!

If you want to go into business and are unsure what it might be, then we can also assume that you have spent a great deal of time in searching for answers. Now when we add the pressure of making sure your business is innovative and different the problem becomes one that seems unsolvable. Most of us try to hammer away at a problem until we find a partial solution or, failing that, we give up. The forceful approach may produce results, but often at the cost of stress and unhappiness at not finding an answer. Instead of worrying about the many possibilities in any situation, *just let go*. Forget the problem, set it aside with the mental promise to come back. You are not giving up, you are leaving the solution to a particular outcome to your inner most consciousness while you let go of the conscious demand for an answer. But letting go of anxious striving can be a perplexing thing. We all want assurance that whatever situation we are in will have a satisfactory outcome. Letting go does not promise that. It is much like the story of the boy who was thrown into deep water by his father and told, "Now learn to swim." He was frightened, and in a state of panic. He could not touch the bottom. But suddenly he found that by kicking his legs and moving his arms he could stay afloat, and he was swimming. Before this, he could not learn to swim because he feared the water and had doubts about his own abilities. By being thrown into the water he was forced to let go of these fears and doubts and do something that would keep him afloat. Sometimes we accumulate so much baggage of reasons, doubts and fear of being different that we build barriers to accomplishing our goals.

Have you ever had the experience of trying hard to remember something important and it just will not come to you? Then, when you are doing something totally unrelated to that problem the thing you were trying to remember pops into your head. You gave up trying to remember. You did everything you could to bring that memory back and the harder you tried the more frustrated you became until the stress of the situation simply closed down your memory bank. Giving up on the problem and concentrating on something else caused the stress to disappear and the memory bank to become clear.

If you are trying to figure out what kind of business will be best for you. It needs to be a business that will utilize some of your skills and background, and certainly one that will fit your particular life style. First, let us take some things you *should not do*. Do not ask anyone who has a particular agenda or motive for directing you one way or the other. You should not counsel with a banker, an insurance person, a business broker or counselor or a person who has never been in business. This will include friends and work associates. You can discuss your business with these people later on but right now you need ideas, not direction. I recommend that you arrange to talk to a person who has been in business for at least ten years. Or, a person who has successfully owned several businesses. You will find these people very willing to share their experiences with you and to give you good practical advice. Just make sure that person is not going to be a competitor.

Once you "jump in" and begin to collect data on your own an idea of the perfect business will appear to you. It is at this point that you need to include your family in the decision process, keeping in mind that in many cases the family may not share your enthusiasm as we previously discussed.

Assuming that you have managed to extract yourself from the "box" we mentioned earlier, and have adopted an entrepreneurial perspective about your business, the question becomes, "how can I make this business different?" Here again, you have to let go and not become bogged down in doubts, pleasing others or fitting in. Look at your competition with a complimentary eye. What are they doing that is innovative and is this why they are successful? What is the passion and the essence of their business? Then, who will your potential customers be? Talk to them and ask what they would like to see changed in that product or service. We will discuss this at length in Chapter Six.

Chapter Three Summary Quiz.

1. What is Innovation and how will it affect your decision to start a business?
2. What kind of support can you expect initially from your family and friends?
3. How do you make your business different from others doing the same thing?
4. Why is the ability to listen important to your business, and how do you develop good listening skills?
5. Identify at least five successful business people with whom you plan to discuss your business idea?

Assignment: Go back to pages 23-24 and follow the "Observational Skills" directions. This is a one week exercise.

Chapter Four

What Kind of Business is Right for You?

> *"Success is getting what you want, Happiness is wanting what you get"*
>
> Dorothy Stevenson

In this chapter we will discuss the business identification process and how to select a business that is right for you *because it is critical to your success that there is a perfect fit.*

Entrepreneurial drive and personal characteristics are important to making a business successful, but if you are in a business that is a wrong fit for you, or involves something in which you do not have a burning interest, you might as well stay where you are and not open the doors of your business in the first place.

Have you ever noticed that when a son or daughter takes over a successful business that was started by their father that it will often suffer from lack of attention or worse it may fail because the desire that built the business is not there? The father had the drive, determination and passion. The heirs do not so the business is taken for granted and slowly dies. The same analogy applies to starting a business that does not have your total dedication and interest. This also applies to your wife or husband. They must also share your passion or they become a detriment to your success. We can refine this even further and say that the business must fit your goals and temperament and those of your wife or husband. If you are not totally in love with the idea of this business being a main part of your life then you are starting out with three strikes against you.

It may seem a bit overwhelming to have decided that you want to be in business but have no idea of the best business for you. Believe me, a lot of successful business owners were in the same predicament at one time. Interviews of these people suggest that their selection of a business simply came from lots of research. They will tell you that you need to begin reading popular business magazines like INC and Entrepreneur. You need to identify an area of interest that represents your experiences, hobbies, likes and dislikes. Pick a general area then begin researching businesses that serve that area.

Then, even when you have narrowed it down to one or two possible businesses, you will hit a roadblock; something that keeps you from taking that first crucial step. Maybe it is the fear of the unknown, failure or even success. Then there will be those who are just overwhelmed by the thought of starting from scratch. They think they have to start with an empty slate and then figure out "what kind of product or service do I need to invent? The good news is that you don't have to re-invent the wheel. The opportunities are out there, all you have to do is look at similar businesses and see what they are doing and say to yourself " what can I do to make it better," or, " what kind of creative innovation can I add to that business that they do not have." If this seems daunting, then maybe buying an existing business or a franchise will be best for you.

Starting from Scratch

Unless you are a technological genius, trying to re-invent the wheel is a big waste of time, if you are another Bill Gates or Steve Jobs, then maybe so. But for most of us it is a matter of answering the question: "How can I do something better and how can I do it differently that the other guy?" On a broader scale, paying attention to current trends while trying to predict future trends can help you identify a market just waiting for a business.

Then, there are those inspiring moments that most of us have had at one time or another. Have you ever thought: "I wish someone would invent something, or improve something to take care of this?" That was the very thought that Tomina Edmark had when she was fixing her hair one day. She was a marketing representative for IBM. One night, she went to see a movie and she noticed a woman in the audience sporting a unique hairstyle. When she got home she tried to replicate the style, but her efforts led to frustration. She looked around the house trying to find something that would make her hair stay in place. The moment of inspiration came when she found a pair of knitting needles, cut them in half and taped them together. She stuck the thing in her hair and it worked. She had just invented the Topsy Tail, a small plastic device with a loop on the end that you stick in your hair to create a pony tail with a French twist. Now why (and sometimes you don't question it) she thought that anybody else would care is the big question. But she did. So she placed mail order ads in magazines just to see if anyone would buy one. When Glamour Magazine ran an article about Topsy Tail it generated $100,000 worth of orders in just three weeks. She realized she could get even more orders if she had an instructional video, demonstrating how to use her product. She sent her product to several TV infomercial production companies. She contracted with one of the companies and an infomercial was born. It demonstrated how to use the product. You got the Topsy Tail and an instruction book for $12.95. When sales started booming the Topsy Tail was sold retail for $9.95 without the book. Her take from the infomercial in just three months was $30 million in sales.

What lesson did we learn here?

1. That the best possibilities come from everyday things that can either be an improvement to something or a new thing that we have improvised on our own. How many things have you improvised to meet an immediate need?
2. She did not stop when she found the solution, but thought other women may have the same problem, so why not look into it?
3. She spent the money to have someone make the Topsy Tail devices and then spent more money to have them advertised. Many people would not go this far, and it is this willingness to take the risk that separates the entrepreneurs from the rest. She had to borrow about $10,000. to do this.
4. She convinced Glamour Magazine that her Topsy Tail was news worthy and was fortunate to have them run an article about it. The article and an ad that went with it paid off and she was on the way.
5. Using the infomercial was a great idea. TV stations that broadcast infomercials usually take a percentage of the mail orders that come to the station, so she was only out the cost of the video production. This did not bother her because she knew there was a market based on the results of the Glamour magazine results.
6. Bottom line: Perseverance, willingness to take a risk, and planning.

While Edmark's business idea originated from a particular problem, there are others that originate from observation of things that can be made better.

John Osher was standing in the cashier's line at a supermarket when he noticed a little girl twirling a lollipop in her mouth. Osher thought: "why not make a small electric motor that will twirl the lollipop so the child won't have to?" He went home and took apart a couple of his son's toys that had little motors in them and invented Twirl-e-Pop. He found a company that would make them for him and a marketing company that would promote them. The idea was a tremendous success, netting Osher a lot of money. He is also the one who decided that the tooth brush would be better if it had a little electric motor that would twirl the brushes. A large tooth paste company ran a test market for him at less that $7.00 each where the closest competitor was Braun with a $60.00 electric brush. In a test market they exceeded their projections in less than six months. Osher eventually sold his idea to Gillette for several million dollars.

All of this because he has the ability to *observe* things around him and make them better.

How About Experience?

Many people start businesses because of on-the-job experience, a hobby or simply a business they have been thinking about for a long time.

I know a fellow who retired from a large industrial woodworking company. He had been one of their top salesmen for twenty years, and had trained many other salesmen in the tricks and techniques of selling woodworking machinery. Because his company was a leader in the industry, (they only had one competitor), he had done very well and retired at age 60 with a large retirement savings account. His passion was cabinet making. It had been his hobby for many years, so he thought: "That is the kind of business I would like to start." He set up a small shop and began contacting builders. Being a salesman this was easy for him to do. He got orders, not for custom made cabinets, but for low quality production cabinets. It seems builders were more interested in fast installation and high margins than they were in quality. Fortunately he did not have a lot of money invested in equipment, so when he decided that the market for custom cabinets was not what he wanted he was not hurt financially. About this time he had an opportunity to buy a wood pallet manufacturing business that was for sale. The two partners who owned it could not get along. He knew about this business because he had sold them machinery a few years back. He negotiated a good buy-out and was suddenly in the wood pallet making business, with six employees and a list of customers. His background in the woodworking industry served him well and his sales ability enabled him to double sales within six months. Acknowledging that his greatest weakness was accounting, he hired a full time bookkeeper and appointed one of his men as Plant Foreman. This enabled him to devote his time to his strong suit–sales. By the end of his first year his sales had increased to $2.5 Million and 16 employees, from the $750,000. and six employees when he bought the business.

This success story has four main points: First, he stayed with what he knew; sales and the wood industry. Second, he was not afraid to back out of his first business when it did not appear to have a future, and before he suffered a great loss. Third, he was astute in seeing that an opportunity existed where others were giving up. He was able to take advantage of the partner's dilemma, and turn it into an opportunity for himself. Fourth, he recognized his own weaknesses in running the business and hired people who could help him. What is not apparent is that he had an attorney carefully analyze the sales contract before he bought the business, and he had a CPA analyze the financials of the business. The same attorney and CPA then structured the new business for him. He was assured that existing problems were remedied and the path was cleared for him to conduct his business and to grow.

Could he have started a pallet manufacturing business from scratch? Yes, because his background was in the wood industry and he understood it, but fortunately he did not have to. This case is pertinent because it demonstrates how a person's background can become a tremendous asset in making a business successful.

Let's assume that like my friend you have experience in the business you want to start, what is the next step?

Identify your business objectives: Remember? In the first chapter you were asked to identify *personal goals*? What do you want to accomplish in owing your own business? Is it making money, or something else? What motivates you the most? Some people start businesses simply to leave their mark; the business is not only a means of making a living, but a way of creating something that bears their personal stamp. **Creativity** comes in many forms; from designing a new thing, to devising a new process, or even a new way to make sales, or to handle customers.

Control is often a goal because we simply want more control over our lives. Control is a major motivator, often more important than money because we think it will result in more time with our families, communities, or hobbies. But control has two sides: you need to be at the business to exercise control–businesses do not run by themselves, and you can over-control, which is detrimental to the growth of the business.

If you are starting a business it is obvious that you like a **Challenge.** You are likely to be a problem solver and a risk taker, enjoying the task of figuring out solutions to problems. People who enjoy challenge can be the most successful business people, but challenges are meant to be solved and it can be detrimental to simply seek out the challenges for self satisfaction..

Every person starting a business wants to make **Money.** Maybe just enough to have a decent income, or enough to totally change your way of living with another house at the beach and a ski lodge in Aspen. How much you want or need affects how you will develop your business. Will you need investors? Will you give up control to grow the business quickly?

Following worksheet that gives you an opportunity to examine your business objectives:
In a range of 1 to 4 mark each item as: (1) Extremely important, (2)

Somewhat important, (3) Somewhat important, (4) Not important.

Creativity:

Determining the design or look of a product/packaging   _____
Creating new products or services   _____
Devising new business procedures/policies   _____
Identifying new company opportunities   _____
Creating new business materials   _____
Devising new ways of doing old things   _____

Control:

Over your work responsibilities   _____
Over your time, work hours, etc.   _____
Over Company decisions   _____
Over products or services   _____
Over other employees   _____
Over work environment   _____
Over your future and business future   _____

Challenge:

Long term problem solving   _____
Critical (immediate) problem solving   _____
Handling many issues at one time   _____
Continually dealing with new issues   _____
Developing solutions to product problems   _____
Organizing projects   _____
Managing and keeping employees focused   _____

Money: *(Measure Wealth as equity in the company)*

Income needed immediately   _____
Income needed within one to two years   _____
Income needed in two to five years   _____
Wealth desired in two to five years   _____
Wealth desired in six to ten years   _____

The business objectives of most entrepreneurs can be summed up in these three categories: Creativity, Control, Challenge and Money. We all want each of them to some degree, but knowing which we most want, or need, can help us structure our businesses to best achieve our goals. Keep in mind there are sometimes trade-offs between these goals; staying at the center of the creative process may mean you need to have a partner or to grow slowly; wanting more cash often means having less control, once again trading off control for cash.

Go Back and look at where you have placed the most importance in these categories. Create a sentence for each item where you have placed a number 4. For example if we take just the first item in each category it may look like this:

"It is important to me that my product has outstanding packaging and design and that I have complete control of this responsibility. I will be responsible for all long term problems and I will need immediate income".

Obviously, this is not a good business model. The important thing is that this exercise gives us an opportunity to look at our objectives in a different light. I suggest that you also construct a sentence for each number; all the threes, twos and ones, just for comparison.

Product or Service?

In Chapter 11, you will find a step-by-step description of the process involved in starting a Service, Manufacturing, Retail, Wholesale or E-Commerce business. The main thing we will stress in this section is the importance of planning. The accent is on being prepared and eliminating surprises. You will also find that every business has a need for establishing solid relationships with attorneys, accountants, bankers and vendors. These people are actually your "external" board of advisors and you cannot make good decisions without them.

Attorneys:

When your business idea becomes a reality because your market research proves you have a viable opportunity, the first person you will contact is a good business attorney. He or she will help you determine whether you need to be a sole proprietor or a corporation of some kind, and will prepare the papers required and file them with the Secretary of State. The attorney will also make sure that your annual corporate minutes are kept up to date.

Accountant:

I recommend a CPA who specializes in business. This person will help you set up your books and instruct you regarding the many accounting procedures that govern your business. He or she will make it easy for you, and if you follow the procedure I recommend in Chapter 9, you can minimize the cost and the visits to your CPA. This person will also help you prepare the financial information you will need if you prepare a business plan. Equally important, your CPA will prepare your quarterly, mid year and annual tax returns for you. I do not recommend that you try to do this yourself. You run your business and let the CPA take care of the financial and tax side of the business.

Banker:

You will probably have a long term relationship with your banker. Therefore it is very important that he or she is a person that you get along with; one who respects you and is interested in your business. Keep in mind that your account with the bank is important and it is in their best interest that as your business grows and prospers your deposits will increase. The banker is the person to whom you will present your business plan, and the presentation of the plan will be your second meeting with him. The first meeting is actually when you are scouting for a banker you like. When you find him or her you will introduce yourself and state that you are starting a business and are interested in finding a bank. Do not have your business plan with you at this meeting, but you should mention that you have one and ask if he would like to see it. If you are interested in a loan to get your business started do not mention it at this first meeting. Get an appointment to come in the next day to talk to him or her, and this time bring your business plan. Determine if the bank is a "Preferred Lender" this is a designation by the SBA that allows a bank to process an SBA loan internally. Non-Preferred Lenders are required to send the loan application to the SBA, and it takes weeks, sometimes months, to get it back. You can call the SBA on their 800 number and ask who the Preferred Lenders are in your area.

Vendors:

You cannot live without them if you are in a manufacturing, retail or wholesale business. Therefore you need to select the vendors from whom you will be buying your products early in the planning process. Go visit them; tell them what your business in and how they can help; ask about pricing, terms, delivery and special discounts. Keep in mind that at this point they do not know you and may be cautious about start-up businesses. If they do extend credit it will be based on YOUR credit history and not the business you are starting. This is why it is so important to make sure your credit history is good. Notice that they will have you fill out a credit application–just as you will when you have charge customers–and it will ask for the names of suppliers from whom you are currently buying. Of course you don't have any because you are just starting your business. They are not interested in department stores or service stations, so they will ask for your personal bank account number and your social security number. With this, they will find your credit score and determine if your banking history is stable. If it all looks good the vendor will extend credit to you. After you have been in business for two to three years, and your business has a positive cash flow, vendors will charge to your business, but even then, you will be asked to personally guarantee payment of purchases.

One interesting thing about vendors: there are many cases where a vendor will finance a start-up business because that business will buy the bulk of their inventory from them; they can maintain a lien on the inventory, and they have checked you out and feel you will be successful. They can also send customers to you and give advice on marketing.

Sources of Information:

Small Business Administration
(Excellent site)   *www.sba.gov*
U.S. Department of Commerce,
Bureau of the Census: *www.census.gov/epcd*
2002 Economic Census
(Survey of Business Owners)   *www.census.gov/econ/2002.html*
Center for Economic Studies (CES)   *www.ces.census.gov*
Business Employment Dynamics: *www.bls.gov/bdm/home.htm*
General Small Business Information   *www.smallbizsearch.com*

An extensive list of Web based information sources is found in Appendix A

Chapter Four Summary Questions:

1. Select a business similar to the kind you want to start and explain how you would improve it.
2. What are the advantages of "Starting from scratch"? The disadvantages?
3. What personal characteristics are necessary to take a new idea to market?
4. How does experience in what you plan to do give you an advantage?
5. Identify the professional advisors you will have, (by name if possible).

First Assignment: Go back to pages 32-33 and do the "Business Objectives" exercise.

Second Assignment: Go to your favorite section of Lowes or Home Depot and select an item that appeals to you. Now, describe how you would improve it.

Chapter Five

Buying an Existing Business or Franchise

If you buy an existing business are you buying the seller's problems? Is buying a franchise about the same as paying a franchisor to work for them? Both questions will be answered in this chapter.

Buying an Existing Business:

"Buyer Beware," is the key to buying a business that someone else has started. This mantra even applies to big corporate mergers and acquisitions. Except in those cases where hundreds of attorneys, merger specialists, bankers and CPAs are involved to make sure investors and stockholders are protected. However, that is not our concern here. We are more interested in knowing what to look for, and look out for, in buying a business some one wants to sell.

Buyers and sellers both seek answers to the same question: "What is this business worth?" Some see the worth of a business as the total dollar value of equipment, fixtures, inventory, buildings and land. The problem is that the sum of these values does not equal the value of the business. What about management, employees, customers and vendors? All of these things have an accumulated value in the business. What about the seller's motivation? Why is he or she selling the business?

While these things are important they have value only to the extent that they contribute to future profits. The owner may have invested $40,000 in equipment that has now depreciated to $20,000, but it is the *profit potential* that establishes the value of the total business, not the value of the assets. We will discuss valuation techniques later on.

How do you find a business for sale?

If you want to hit the ground running with an established business, and have narrowed your choices to a few types of businesses to consider, what is the selection process? If you are currently working in a small business, is there a chance that it may be available sometime soon? Since you know the inner workings of the business, it might be a good place to start. You probably know all kinds of things that could be done to improve it. If you are a manager in the business it is possible you have talked to the owner about buying the business someday? If not, why not start those discussions now.

There are always businesses for sale in the classified section of the newspaper, but I recommend against these simply because they are predominantly distress or scam situations. Unfortunately there is a "business opportunities racket." It is common in the retail field to advertise a business in the newspaper to attract unwary buyers who are usually inexperienced in running a business. It is not uncommon that a single business can wreck several successive owners through sale and resale to a steady stream of newcomers. Unscrupulous brokers who promote these sales make a commission each time the business changes hands. If you decide to use a broker be sure to check with the Better Business Bureau, your banker, accountant and attorney for recommendations.

Business Brokers:

There are ethical and legitimate business brokers who provide a good service for people who want to buy an existing business. These brokers must take classes and pass examinations to become Certified Business Intermediaries (CBI). To find a reliable broker contact the International Business Brokers Association. Go to www.IBBA.org and click on "Find a Broker."

If you want to avoid the fees of a broker and distrust the classified ads you can often find a business through word of mouth. There are a lot of good opportunities that don't get advertised. Bankers, attorneys and CPAs are all good sources of information because they counsel businesses on a regular basis. You can also contact real estate brokers who often know of businesses for sale.

What do you look for in a business?

Every business has a value and it is up to you and the seller to arrive at a price that is acceptable to both of you. It is important that you are able to recognize the specific details that are the most relevant to arriving at the price. You need enough knowledge to take the information from past sales, personnel and financial records and evaluate the historical performance of the business in order to predict probable future developments. You need objectivity to avoid excess enthusiasm that might blind you to the facts. Don't let emotions cloud your decisions.

At a minimum, you need to ask the following questions about the business:
1.   How long have they been in business?

      A.   Who founded it?

      B.   How many owners has it had?

      C.   Why have others sold out?

2.   What is the profit record?

      A.   Is profit increasing or decreasing?

      B.   What are the reasons for increase or decrease?

3.   What is the condition of the inventory, are the goods new or obsolete. You need percentage here: What percent is current and what is obsolete.

4.   Is the equipment in good condition?

      A.   Who owns it? Are there any liens against it?

      B.   How does it compare with competitors equipment.

      C.   If leased, how long does the lease run.

          1. Is it a capital or operational lease?

          2. What are the conditions?

          3. Can the lease be renewed?

5.   Are the sources (vendors) of supply dependable?

6.   What about future and present competition?

      A.   Are new competitors or substitute materials or methods visible on the horizon?

7.   What is the condition of the area around the business; are traffic routes or parking regulations likely to change?

8.   Why does the present owner want to sell?

      A.   Where will he or she go?

      B.   What do customers, suppliers, local people think of the present Owner and the business?

It is important that you understand how the value of a business is determined before you ever enter into negotiations for the business.

What is the historical (at least three years) financial record?

If you are good at analyzing financial statements, fine, you can do this part yourself. If not, have your CPA do it for you. This is the most important part of the valuation process if you are thinking about selling or buying a business. If buying a business, you need to know if the income from the business will be satisfactory for you and your family and if not what can be done to improve it. You need to compare the operating ratios for the business with those of the industry in order to detect potential problems. We will talk more about ratios later on.

If the owner of the business says he or she does not have financial statements then BEWARE. Financial statements are an integral part of running a business because they detail where the business stands and are a tool through which management makes decisions. You cannot make intelligent decisions without them. The absence of financial statements means the owner has something to hide, and you need to run from that situation as fast as you can.

Another indicator of a bigger problem is when the owner of the business says the reason the financial statements show the business has no profit is because he or she has "purposely" maintained a negative profit to keep from paying taxes. Sometimes the owner will wink while telling you this as if to say I'm making a lot of money I do not want to show on the financials. The truth is that the business is not making money; the owner is lying and this is another reason to run as fast as you can.

The third danger sign is if the owner has prepared his or her own financial statements. "Why should I pay a CPA when I can prepare them myself?" This leads to all kinds of manipulation. Banks will not accept "home grown" statements and neither should you.

Types of Financial Statements.

We go into detail about financial statements in Chapter 9. But for our purpose here, there are three types of statements: *Audit, Review and Compilation*. The difference between them is based on who bears responsibility for the accuracy of the information used to create the statement. In the audited statement the CPA bears the responsibility for the collection and presentation of information. As a result the CPA wants the information to be very accurate and will dig into every aspect of the business. This takes a lot of time and as a result the audited statement is very expensive. In the Compilation and Review Statements, the CPA depends on the business owner to provide information from journals and daily reports, so the owner bears the responsibility for accuracy. In these two, the CPA will include a disclaimer letter as the first page of the statements which says the CPA has no responsibility for the accuracy of information as it was provided by the owner of the business. Obviously, the cost to prepare these statements is much less than the audited statement. As a rule, you will not need audited statements, nor should you require them. A compilation or review statement will provide all the information you will need.

What Else do You Need?

Remember, you are thinking of buying a business someone else has started and developed. They know everything and you need to find out as much as you can in order to make an intelligent decision. If the shoe was on the other foot and you are the one selling the business you would want everything about the business to be as straightforward and open as possible, so you should expect the same if you are the buyer.

In addition to at least three years of financial statements and tax returns here are some other things to check:

1. Has the business employed the same number of people over the past three years? Anticipating a sale, an owner may cut back on employees to boost profits.

2. Maintenance on equipment, vehicles or the buildings can be cut to increase short term profits.

3. Insufficient write-offs of bad debts, inventory shortages, obsolescence and un er depreciation of the firm's fixed assets can also overstate profits

4. Ask to see the business tax returns for the past three years. You may be more comfortable having your CPA do this because it will require a lot of interpretation. If everything is legitimate the owner will not hesitate. However, if the owner refuses to do this he or she may have something to hide.

5. Compare bills and receipts with sales tax receipts. Reconcile past purchases with sales and mark-up claimed. Make certain all back taxes have been paid. Make sure that interest payments and other current obligations are up to date.

Realize that the financial information that you need to analyze the business is sensitive information to the seller, especially if you do not know each other. You can decrease his suspicions about using this information to aid a competing business or some other improper use by agreeing to sign a letter of confidentiality that his attorney can prepare. Following is a sample letter stating your willingness to sign a confidentiality statement:

John Smith, Owner and President
Smith Hardware and Supplies, Inc.

Dear Mr. Smith:

    I want to thank you for the time you spent with me last week regarding the possible purchase of your business. I am interested to the point that I would like to go to the next step and examine your financial records for the past three years. I would also like to see the company tax returns for the same periods of time.

    I know that this information is highly confidential and that you would logically be concerned about improper use of this information. I assure you that I request this information strictly for the purpose of making a purchase decision and the terms of the deal. The only persons with whom I will discuss this information are my attorney, my banker and my accountant. I will also obtain signed confidentiality agreements from them.

    I will return all of your records and any copies made within two weeks. Thank you for your trust. I will not violate it and look forward to continuing this transaction.

Sincerely,
Ralph Jones

Know Exactly What You are Buying.

Earlier in this section I mentioned that we would discuss financial ratios. Whether you are buying or selling a business, ratios are important because they give you a way to see how you are doing compared with others in the same business. Why is this important? Because well run, profitable businesses have ratios that set the standard for the industry you are in. Assuming that you would also like to be profitable, knowing these ratios gives you a basis of comparison. For example: say that a well run business like yours, or the one you want to buy, has a *current ratio* of three to one. That means for every dollar they have in liabilities they have three dollars in assets. That would suggest a healthy business because if they had to pay off all their current liabilities they would have the ability to do so. On the other hand, if the current ratio is one to one, it means they can barely pay their liabilities and have nothing left over. Needless to say, if the current ratio is negative two to one it means they cannot pay off their liabilities and the business is in bad shape. You would not want to buy a business like that, nor would you want your business to be in that condition.

There are all kinds of ratios in business that I will cover in Chapter Nine.

One more word about establishing a value for the business.

Let's face it, after you have studied and compared the ratios and studied the financials and compared these with industry standards, you still need to find the real value of the business whether you are the buyer or the seller. This is something that business brokers do very quickly with specialized computer programs. There are two basic methods of determining the value of a small business. The preferred method is based on expectations of future profits and return on investment. It forces the buyer and seller to give attention to such factors as trends in sales and profits, capitalized value of the business and expectancy of return on investment. This method gives the buyer a chance to compare his investment return in the business to the interest he can get from the money market; a stock, bond or high yielding security. The second method is based on the appraised value of the assets at the time of negotiation, and assumes that these assets will continue to be used in the business. This method gives little consideration to the future of the business. Unfortunately, it is the more commonly used because it is easier

Finalizing the Purchase

After you have thoroughly investigated the business using the tools I have outlined in Chapter Nine, and you have decided to make the owner an offer, you will need to negotiate the terms of the deal and prepare for the closing.

Let's assume you have agreed on a price for the business and the terms of the sale need to be negotiated. Few buyers can write a check for the full amount and the reality is that a lump sum payment may not be in the buyer's or the seller's best interest. For example, the seller may have negative tax implications in a lump sum payment, so selling on installments may be best. Also, by building installment payments into your own financial projections you may find that the business can be paid for out of earnings. Installments assure the seller that his investment in the business will be returned on a tax deferred basis as opposed to paying all the taxes on the sale at one time.

A seller can also make the business more affordable by adjusting the assets. For example, you can ask the seller to sell off excess inventory. He can also factor the accounts receivable, or assume responsibility for all accounts as of the day he sells you the business. If a building and equipment is involved in the sale, the seller can lease these things to you on a separate agreement. The buyer has less to borrow and the seller receives a steady rental income.

Closing the Deal

When you and the seller have reached an agreement, several conditions need to be met to assure a smooth, legal transaction. I recommend using a settlement attorney who can act as a neutral party to draw up the necessary documents. He or she can represent both parties. You simply agree on aclosing date, after all the conditions of the sale have been met such as financing by the buyer and a legal search to determine if there are any liens against the assets. Many states have what is called a "bulk sales law" which obligates the seller to send a letter to all vendors with whom he is doing business, including banks and lessors, announcing that he is selling the business to you and that he has responsibility for all financial and legal activity up to the date of the sale. The seller provides you with that list and the letter and is then legally responsible for any and all activity prior to the sale. Even if he forgets to include a vendor on the list and that vendor comes to you two months after the business is sold to you saying you owe him money for something the seller bought from him, the seller will be legally responsible to pay that bill under the Bulk Sales Law. If you did not have the "Bulk Sales Agreement" you would have to pay such debts.

Another safeguard is an "Escrow Settlement," where the buyer deposits the money and the seller provides the bill of sale and terms of the agreement to an escrow agent. Most banks and other financial institutions have escrow departments. The job of the escrow agent is to hold the money and

all the documents of the sale until proof is shown that all conditions of the sale are satisfied. When all the conditions are met, the escrow agent releases the money to the seller.

> *Knowledge is power, and the more you know about a business or a franchise the better your chances of avoiding problems.*

How About a Franchise?

There are over 2500 different franchises for you to choose from. Like anything else, some are great and many are just one level above being scams. Back in the mid-1950s the Federal Trade

Commission got fed up with the number of complaints they were getting from people who had been taken by unscrupulous franchisors so they passed a law that said every franchisor must fully disclose everything about their program to prospective franchisees. This came out in the form of a lengthy document called the "Uniform Franchise Offering Circular." (UFOC). It is difficult to read and often requires the help of an attorney, but it does provide a remedy by making it extremely difficult for the bad guys to offer a franchise. Keep in mind, every franchise program in the United States must have a UFOC, and it you are interested in a franchise then they are obligated by law to give you one within 10 days of a personal meeting or 10 days before any agreements are signed. Read it and fully understand what you are getting into before signing anything.

Franchise programs are ideal for people who like organizational structure and the management philosophies of those in charge of the program. Very often, people who have worked for a large corporation for many years find that the structure of a franchise is perfect for them. They can enjoy the autonomy of "having their own business" yet find comfort in having someone show them how it is done and supplying everything they need to make it work. These are all things they would have to create if they start from scratch. So the franchise concept is to put you into a business that has a proven system of operation, the right to use their trademark, an identified market, a source of supplies, a training program in which you will learn business techniques and a complete advertising package.

> *There is a saying about franchising that it puts you in business "for yourself, but not by yourself."*

Finding the right franchise is the key. It is like starting your own business because you need to know the strengths an weaknesses of the franchisor, and you need to find the one that compliments your background, interests and long term objectives. Surely, out of 2500 franchise programs there is one for you.

Do Your Homework

I recommend that you get the Entrepreneur magazine list of 500 top franchise programs, because they detail all of the costs and requirements. Then you can check out the International Franchise Association web site at www.franchise.org. I also recommend that you attend one of the big franchise trade shows in a major city. There is even a franchise that sells franchises. It is called The Entrepreneur Source. www.theesource.com. In other words do your homework before letting a fast talking franchise salesperson sell you an unhappy situation.

If you go to a franchise show, or "exposition," as they are often called, there are some things you need to do to prepare:

1. Before you go give considerable thought to really what you are looking for in a franchise. Franchises are expensive, so this deserves some study. For example, are you looking for full time or part time? What kind of business do you think you would enjoy?

2. How much money do you have set aside to purchase a franchise? The list of franchises in Entrepreneur Magazine will tell you how much you will need for the up-front franchisee fee, equipment and leasehold improvements and initial operating expenses.

3. When you go to the show act like a business person. Dress conservatively, bring your spouse but not the kids, take business cards if you have them. Show the franchise representatives that you are a serious prospect.

4. When you arrive at the show pick up a map of the exhibits and study it. Mark the franchisesthat look interesting to you. If it is a large show it can be intimidating and it is a good idea to map out what you want to see in advance. Here is a suggested list of questions:

   A. What is the total investment?
   B. Describe a typical day in the life of a franchisee.
   C. What arrangements are in place for product supply? Do you have a central warehouse or regional warehouses, and how fast is delivery?
   D. Is financing available from the franchisor?

5. Be sure to ask for a copy of the company's UFOC. They probably will not have copies to hand out at the show, but they should take your name and promise to mail one to you *it's the law*. Some franchises will tell you that if you make a good faith deposit of say $1000. they will mail one to you with the promise that if you are not interested they will refund your deposit. This is really stretching the letter of the law, and I would steer clear of a franchise that does this.

6. Collect handout information and business cards from all the franchises that interest you. Sort it out when you get home and write down questions on each one.

7. Finally, this experience should help to narrow down your selection of the best programs for you. Make a list of important questions that will help you make a final decision and call the franchise representative.

As you begin to investigate franchises in which you are interested you will accumulate a pile of promotional material prepared by professional marketing firms. Do not make your decision based on these slick promotions or the calls you will receive from franchise representatives. You need to do your own investigation. In addition to going on-line as previously mentioned, visit your local library and ask the Reference Desk to help you in checking out a specific franchise. You may also want to check with the consumer affairs department in your state, generally associated with the office of Secretary of State. Find out if there have been any bankruptcies or lawsuits and try to determine the nature of the lawsuits. Did they involve fraud or violations of the Federal Trade Commission (FTC)? You can also call the Better Business Bureau in your area to see if complaints have been filed against the company.

What Happens once you have Selected a Franchise?

Once you have selected the franchise you want, you will pay an initial franchise fee, and you will agree to pay on-going royalties on sales to the franchisor, plus advertising fees. In return, you will receive on-going support from the franchisor. When you sign the franchise agreement you will agree to follow their system of doing business and to sell their products or services. The franchise "Operations Manual" is the Bible of the franchise and you will be required to use it. Their explanation is that they have a proven way to sell and by following the procedure in the Manual you will be successful. They want to maintain their brand name and uniformity of product. A good example is McDonald's. Customers know what they are getting whether they are in Indianapolis or London. As a result, a new McDonald's location has a head start compared to an independent hamburger joint.

Perhaps the most significant advantage of buying a franchise is that you get a proven system of operation and training in how to use it. As a franchisee you can avoid many of the mistakes you would make in a start-up because the franchisor has perfected the daily routine as a result of their own trial and error. A reputable franchisor will do all the marketing research so you can feel confident that there is a demand for your product or service when you open your doors. Lack of adequate market research is one of the biggest mistakes made by independent entrepreneurs.

The franchisor will also provide you with a complete picture of your competition, and tell you how to differentiate yourself from them. In effect, you hit the ground running.

Another big advantage of owning a franchise is the strength in numbers you enjoy by being part of a big program. Because of this buying power you will receive substantial discounts on many things essential to your business such as advertising, supplies and services, even negotiating for locations and lease terms. Some suppliers will not deal with a new independent business because it has not proven itself. Often in leasing the right location the franchisor will sign the lease as a guarantor and negotiate favorable terms for the franchisee. Many franchisors will negotiate and guarantee SBA loans if the franchisee does not have adequate start-up capital.

One last tip: call as many of the franchisees listed in the UFOC as you can, then select at least six of them to visit. Here is what you need to find out:

1. Was the training provided by the franchisor helpful in getting started, and is there follow-up training?
2. Is the franchisor responsive to your needs; do they really care about your success or are they just interested in collecting royalties?
3. Describe a typical day or week and if the Operations Manual is helpful in handling specific issues?
4. How many problems have you encountered that you did not anticipate?
5. Do you think the investment and cost information shown in the UFOC is realistic?
6. Generally, are all franchisees happy with the program; are any of them thinking about a class action suit against the franchisor?
7. Have sales and profits met your expectations? (See if they will go into detail about their finances).
8. Does the franchisor force you to open new locations, and threaten to let another franchisee into your territory if you don't?
9. Does the franchisor require a full franchisee fee if you want to open another store? (They should not).
10. Ask the franchisee if they knew what they know now, if they would make the investment again?

Chapter Five Summary Questions.

1. If you wanted to find a business to buy what steps would you take?
2. What are some of the danger signs in a business that is for sale?
3. What "tools" do you have to evaluate a business?
4. How do you find a good franchise?
5. What is the purpose of a UFOC?
6. Why would you select a franchise over buying a business or starting from scratch?

Assignment: If you are interested in a franchise go back to pages 43-44 and answer the questions.

Chapter Six

First, Look at Your Market

Okay, you do not want to buy a business or a franchise because you have a great business idea and have elected to start it from scratch. Besides, why should you pay fees and royalties to work for someone else?

It is a well known fact in business that if you don't have a product or service that people want, then you do not have a business. That means the first thing you have to do, once you have a business in mind, is to determine if there is a market for your product. Seems logical right?, but there are thousands of new business owners who start up every year assuming that people will beat a path to their doors just because a few friends, or the family, tells them it's a good idea. Scientists and engineers are notorious for inventing something that solves a problem only to find there is no market for it. The patent will expire on the shelf. On the other hand the entrepreneur will see an opportunity, then study the market to see if anyone will buy the product. If a thorough market study convinces him or her that it will sell, then he or she will build a product. Remember the story about John Osher in Chapter Four? He invented the Twirly-Pop only after extensive market study told him people would buy a lollipop turned by a little motor. He made millions of dollars as a result.

Many times people with business ideas will be told the first thing they have to do is write a business plan before anything else. This is wrong, simply wrong. The very first thing you have to do is see if your business idea will sell, and you do this by market research. Tedious? Yes, but essential to the success of your business. And, the market research you do can become part of your business plan later on.

Is market research something you should have a consulting firm do for you? The short answer is no, you can do it yourself. First of all you probably cannot afford the cost of having a Marketing or Public Relations firm do it for you, and second, doing the research yourself gives you a "hands on" feel that you will not get by having it done by an outside consulting firm.

What is Market Research?

It is a way of collecting information that will help you identify who will buy your product and how to solve or avoid marketing problems. It helps you identify certain segments within a market that you want to target and to create your own identity. Market research can also help you choose the best geographic location for your business. Also, this is the only time you will be able to get close to your competition to find out what they are doing. After you open your doors they will know you are there and are not apt to give you any information.

What is Involved in Market Research?

You will need information from three sources: *the industry you are in; the consumer you will sell to, and your competition.* In researching **the industry you are in** it is important to find out if there is any room left for your business. In other words, "Is the window of opportunity wide open or about to close?" Obviously you don't want to jump into an industry that is saturated with your product or service. How do we find that out? The best source is a trade association, and there is a trade association for every conceivable business. Go to the business reference desk your local library and ask for the "**Encyclopedia of Trade Associations**," (Gale Research). There may be several of them for your industry, so select one that seems to be the largest and call their 800 number. Or, you can do a Google search for your trade association on the internet. When you call, tell them you are researching the statistics and growth in the industry, and what areas of the industry seem to be expanding. You will also need to find out if the industry is catering to new customers; what technological developments are being created and how you can use this to your advantage.

A word about trade associations in general: They depend on memberships to exist, so don't be surprised if they refuse to give you information unless you first join. Contact several of them, select the best one and be prepared to spend some membership money. The greatest service trade associations offer their members is the collection and summarization of all kinds of information. For example, most of them will show combined summaries of common size balance sheets and revenue statements by region. This is extremely important to you in the development of projections for your business plan. A trade association will also analyze industry trends, provide lists of their members and preferred suppliers, some of whom will give you a discount because you are a member. The better trade associations will have annual conventions where their members can get together; meet vendors, view products and attend important seminars.

The customer you will sell to is the key to your success so you need to know as much about him or her as you possibly can. Your customer research should start with a survey. This will help you to make reasonable forecasts. To do this, you first need to determine the market limits or boundaries within which you will be selling. This is followed by studying the spending characteristics of the customers in this area. Do you have to do this yourself? No, it has already been done for you, and all you have to do is go to your local library. Ask at the Reference Desk for the *U.S. Statistical Abstract.* It contains a lot of social and economic information. Then check out the *American Demographics* magazine which contains specific consumer information. As long as you are at the Reference Desk tell the librarian exactly what you selling and what you are looking for in a customer profile; income levels, spending habits, and demographics. I have found that a knowledgeable librarian can be a great ally in helping to identify potential customers and where they are located.

Another source, often overlooked, is a good mailing list company. Look in the Yellow Pages under "Mail Lists." There are generally five to eight companies listed, all with 800 numbers. Call them and explain what you are looking for. They will often be able to supply you with a list of potential customers that fit your specifications. I will explain how to get the most out of this list later on.

The last resort in surveying your customers is to pay a marketing consulting firm to do it for you. This can be very expensive depending on the amount of detail you want. However it may turn out that they already have the information on file and it may be relatively inexpensive.

Learning about your competition is critical to your success. First it is important to understand that no matter what your business is you have competition and they fall into two groups: Strategic–those who use similar marketing strategies sell similar products and have similar abilities. In this definition every pizza parlor is competing not only for the pizza consumer but for anyone who is willing to spend money in a restaurant. Another way you can group competitors is by the way strongly they compete for the same customer's dollar, and how much of a challenge this will be to you.

Let's put this in perspective. At this point in time your competition does not know you exist or that you plan to go after their customers. You will never have a better time than right now to determine their strengths and weaknesses. It is learning about their weaknesses that will give you a *competitive edge.* For example, if you find out that your major competitor has a poor service reputation, then you will know that good service is what you will promote.

It would be easy to go through the Yellow Pages to pick out who you think your competition is, it would also be inaccurate. If you have completed your research of industry and consumer information then you have a clearer idea of your competition. The point is, do not underestimate the number of competitors. If your business is local or regional you will need to know exactly how many competitors are in the area. If it is national in scope your task is much harder. The analysis you do of your competition should supply a complete picture of their SWOT; that is, Strengths, Weaknesses, Opportunities and Threats. Take a ledger sheet and draw four columns with those four headings. This will be the first step in your competitive analysis. You will be making entries in each of these areas from now on.

Visit your competition as a customer and follow-up with a phone call. Remember, they do not know you plan to be in business soon, so this is to your advantage. Ask questions about things that would be important to you if you were in business, such as pricing, quality, guarantees, service, delivery and inventory. Find out who their suppliers are and if they are happy with them. Later on you will talk to these same suppliers in addition to those recommended by your trade association.

If you are working for a company now that will become your competition when you go into business–Be Careful. If you have a "Non-Compete agreement" it may mean you will have to wait a few years before you can start your business. If you don't have a non-compete agreement you still have to be careful because such things as price lists, customer and vendor lists belong to them and it would be fraudulent for you to physically take them. However, the things that you remember and perhaps have written down on your SWOT ledger are yours.

A client of mine returned from a student trip to Australia convinced that a coffee and donut shop would be very successful there. Having no experience in this business he got a job in Atlanta with a donut franchise after he graduated from college in order to study what they did and why they were so successful. At the time he was told that they had no plans to open stores in Australia. He worked for two months as a server and then six months as a store manager. All the while he took careful notes on every aspect of the store operation. Yes, he did sign a non-compete agreement when he became a manager but because the Franchisee did not plan to franchise in Australia at that time it did not apply. He was completely honest with his boss and with the franchise regarding his plans and when he left it was with their blessings and good wishes. He returned to Australia and after considerable hassle with the government about being a non-citizen opening a business, he finally opened his first store. It was very successful and after becoming an Australian citizen he eventually opened ten more stores and is today a multi-millionaire.

I know many business owners who worked for a company just to gain inside knowledge about the business, then opened in competition with them. There is a question of ethics here, but it is such a common practice that it has almost become standard. It is no different than one grocery store sending an employee to another store to check out their prices, or a clothing store checking out their competition to see what fashions or lines they are carrying. You have to stay on top of your competition and these are some of the ways it is done. When you open your business you can count on the competition sending someone over to check out your prices and service. So get ready.

What is Your Market Niche?

This is another way of saying "What makes you different from your competition." It is the "Difference" you will sell, and that plus your competition's weakness is your competitive advantage.

When you promote your business you will be promoting that which makes you different. Look at it another way, if you open a business that is exactly the same as your competition, then why would customers need to do business with you? Maybe you have determined that you will be offering a product or service that is different, and your study of the competition proves that you bring better and faster service; that you have a warranty program they don't have or that the value you bring to your customer is greater than anything they can find. Any of these can create your competitive edge. But the funny thing in business is that as soon as you are "out there" with this advantage, your competition sees what is going on because they are losing customers to you. So logically they will start offering the same thing, or maybe even better.

The point is that competitive advantage is a temporary thing. If this is all you have in your arsenal then your market niche quickly disappears. You must work continuously on product or service improvement in order to stay ahead of your competition. Interestingly, the larger your competition, the slower they will be to react, and sometimes they will simply ignore you because it takes too long to go through all the approvals to change their product. The bureaucracy and levels of management in a big corporation make it difficult for them to respond. A good analogy would be the case of Cellular One. When they started from scratch in the 70s, NYNEX was the largest provider of cellular telephone service on the East coast. They were so large and so popular that no one should have thought about challenging them, but Cellular One did. It is estimated that NYNEX built twice as many towers, (at $400,000 each), spent two to three times as much on advertising and had thousands of employees. Yet, Cellular One grew from scratch to $100 million in sales in just five years and won three customers for every one that NYNEX won. What made the difference? It was outstanding management of resources and superb service. Because they did not have a huge management structure and were able to respond to customers quickly they not only succeeded but they became the dominant cellular phone service in the nation.

The Ideal Customer

Let us assume that at this point you have a great idea for a business; you have compiled all the information you need about your competitors, have a general idea of your customer base and have identified a market niche. Now let's take the next critical step: putting a face and the location of customers who will buy your product. You will either be selling to consumers or to other businesses. Being true to our mantra *"Think big but start small,"* we know that you cannot be all things to all people, so you need to define your target market. You need to find the ideal customer who you know will buy your product. In the beginning smaller is better because having a few loyal customers when you start-up gives you a base to build on. Treating a few good customers extremely well will result in referrals and references, so you need to focus on who they are.

To begin with, your niche is not the same as field you are in. For example the printing business is a field, but printing full color business cards is a niche. A more specific niche may be selling full color business cards to real estate agents. Therefore, after studying your competition you find that the delivery time on these cards is currently seven days. Your experience tells you that with the right equipment you can deliver these cards over night. *That is your competitive edge!* When you promote your product to real estate agents you will emphasize over night delivery. Real estate people hand out a lot of cards and from your market research you have learned that they are constantly running out.

To locate them you will call the local Real Estate Association and find out how you can get a list of all the real estate firms and agents in your area. Then by making up a good looking brochure you will send a personalized letter and the brochure, along with your business card to a select group. Why just a few to begin with? Because you do not know what the response will be and you do not want to get so many orders you cannot deliver overnight as promised. Later on I will discuss advertising techniques and the best way to get guaranteed orders with the right kind of promotion.

This short example illustrates how to identify a market niche and the way to work within its boundaries. Your experience plus your market research are key in determining your niche or market segment, then determining who within that segment is most likely to buy your product is your advantage.

Change is Never Ending.

Remember I said that as soon as your competition realizes you are taking away their customers they will probably begin offering the same thing? Someone is bound to; it may even be an upstart you hadn't counted on. It could even be one of your employees who see that you are doing well and figures he can do it better. You can never tell where it will come from, but you can be assured that it will. The answer is you must constantly review and rework your edge. You cannot rest just because your idea took off like a rocket because rockets come down and you need to be ready. This means constantly watching your competition; constantly studying changes in your market that indicate new products or services, and constantly asking your customers about their requirements. Make your customers your allies, even to the extent of holding mini-seminars for them perhaps with dinner and refreshments so you can stay close to them.

Location.

I refuse to say it three times because it is so overdone. However, its importance cannot be over stated regardless of the type of business you are in. Location is an important part of marketing even if you operate from a home office. The reasons are fairly obvious; you need to be close to your customers, but at what cost? There are other factors in the equation: the type of business you are in, the facilities and resources you will need and accessibility to customers.

Before you start looking for the right location you first need to know exactly what you *must have* and what you would *settle for*; then what you absolutely will not have. The analysis that goes into location selection can be time consuming, but it is essential that you consider every aspect of the search. Keep in mind that many of the start-up decisions you make can be corrected, but location is difficult, maybe impossible to change. Here again, you can hire a marketing consultant to find a location for you but it will be expensive so I don't recommend it. Secondly, do not ask a real estate firm to find a location for you because they will limit a search to properties where they can make a commission. Finally, if you are buying a franchise the franchisor will do the market research and location for you–that is part of your franchisee fee.

There are five possible location considerations: *Retail, Commercial, Home-based, Industrial and Mobile*. Then there are combinations of each of these. For example, commercial can be a warehouse but you operate out of your van or car. The vehicle is your mobile office. Let's look at each possibility:

Retail locations are difficult because you have to be where your customers are, and these locations can be expensive. You do not select a retail location because it is convenient to you. Once you have identified who your customers are and where they are located you then need to begin your search. Selecting a location because it is inexpensive is not advised, because there is a reason it is inexpensive. Selecting an expensive mall location is also a mistake unless you are a franchise or a chain store that demands it. Look at the choices you have. Draw a circle on a map with your ideal location in the center, and then begin your search starting at the center and working outward. Make a list of every possibility whether it has a "for rent" sign on it or not. It may be a free standing building, a shopping mall, strip shopping center, downtown shopping area or mixed use facilities. Shopping malls and strip centers will have the highest cost per square foot and generally the most restrictive lease contracts. They also add on such costs as Common Area Maintenance (CAM) and sometimes a percentage of your sales over a predetermined yearly gross sales figure. On the other hand I have negotiated favorable leases with the owners of new strip centers that were anxious to find tenants, so do not hesitate to talk to the owner of a new strip center. I will discuss lease terms at the end of this chapter.

Commercial locations have even more options than retail. First, commercial office buildings and business parks offer traditional office space for businesses that do not require a lot of walk-in or drive-by traffic. A fairly new concept in office space offers weekly or monthly rates to business people who are getting started and need an attractive address, or sales representatives who need short term space. These "Executive Suites" often provide receptionist and secretarial service along with faxing. copying and conference rooms. If you are absolutely sure of the office location you need be prepared to sign a three year lease. Shorter term leases are proportionately more expensive.

If you need warehouse space and location is not critical, you have a large number of choices. There are strip warehouse/office facilities in every medium to large city in the U.S. They are popular with start-ups because you have a small office in the front and warehouse (or manufacturing) space in the back, with a loading dock and overhead door. In this case, you should find one close to where you live to save driving time. If you need a lot of warehouse space you can find free standing buildings or space you can sub-let in a large warehouse. A word of caution: be sure the space you lease has adequate fire protection with approved walls and sprinkler systems. Otherwise, your insurance premiums will be very high, and in a non-approved warehouse you may not be able to get insurance. Finally, unless you have a good deal of experience in leasing commercial warehouse space I recommend that you hire a commercial real estate professional to do all the pre-screening and negotiating. In this case the landlord typically pays the agent's commission. To find an agent ask your attorney, banker or CPA for a referral.

Home based businesses are the growing trend in our economy because of outsourcing and the internet. Big industry has found it to be less expensive for them to outsource everything from sales and word processing, including graphic arts, to sub-assembly manufacturing. The internet has caused a boom in home businesses with a variety of auction sites like E-bay, multilevel sales programs, and independent marketing businesses. A friend of mine has an equipment leasing business that he operates from his home office and writes an average of $12 million in leases a year. There are stories about home based E-bay businesses grossing millions of dollars in sales. The good thing about these home based businesses is that you don't have to commute to work and if the business fails there are no leases to negotiate. On the negative side room for growth is limited and if you have employees there can be accommodation problems. Also, if you need to meet clients it is not good to meet in your living room, so meet them at your local library or even a restaurant.

Zoning can also be a problem so be sure to check with your city or county zoning office to see if there are any restrictions about running a business in your home. About the only objection I have experienced is a restriction on the number of delivery trucks or cars parked in front of your home.

A lady I know started a very small business in her home making solid silver belt buckles with precious stones in them. At first she made them for friends and relatives at Christmas time, but then others began asking her to sell them one, so suddenly she had a business. She and her attorney husband lived in an affluent neighborhood of Atlanta, but because her sales of buckles and requirements to make them were small, they though nothing about zoning, or even a business license. Her husband felt it was a nice hobby for her. But, as often happens, more and more people began asking to buy her "one of a kind" belt buckles and the business began to grow. One of her customers, a buyer for a large department store, asked her to make several of them and her business took off. The next chapter is this story occurred when her husband came home one night to find several cars parked in their driveway and both garage doors closed. He went in to find five people assembling and packaging belt buckles. That evening he informed his wife that they were in violation of at least three zoning laws and that she would have to stop making buckles. Instead, she leased an office/warehouse unit about three miles from their home and increased production. Keep in mind her market niche was rich people who didn't mind spending $1,200 or more for a belt buckle. The amazing thing is that she could not keep up with the demand. This story is about the effect of zoning on a business, but it does have an epilog. She increased her product line into several high-end jewelry items; now has a factory with over 25,000 square feet of space; employs over 20 people and has sales of $13 million a year.

Industrial locations generally refer to manufacturing or heavy distribution. Business people who are looking for this type of space have experience in the type of manufacturing they will do and the space required. It would be very unusual for someone who has never been in manufacturing to suddenly decide to do so. The point is, if you are looking for manufacturing space you know what you are looking for and you will most likely look in light industrial parks. You will also know if you need a free standing commercial building and if rail or water port access is required. Zoning will be in place and special permits will only be needed if you are dealing with pollutants of any kind.

Mobile. This is hardly a location and I have included it here because there are many people in business for themselves who actually use a vehicle for an office and a delivery vehicle. Their computer and all office needs are located on the front seat of the vehicle, and the trunk of the car or back of the van serves as a storage warehouse for the products they are selling. I have a friend who has his own pest control business. Everything he needs is in his truck. When he comes home at night he simply parks his truck in the driveway. He has a rule that he does not discuss business at the dinner table and does not bring paperwork in to do at home. Every aspect of his business is in his truck.

What is Best for You?

Now that you have determined who your customer is and how best to serve him or her with an appropriate location, we need to look as some other location issues. As I previously mentioned, once you have signed a lease you are stuck with that location even if things go bad for you, so you need to understand leases and how to negotiate them..

Leasing Property

Why would you lease instead of buying property? First, you want to preserve your cash, and leasing is a form of leveraging. Very few people starting a business have the cash to buy property, so leasing is the logical alternative. Even if you have the money to purchase land, building and equipment there is a question of where it is best placed; in the business, such as inventory, promotion and sales or research and development, or in property. Most experts agree, invest in the business not in property. In effect, leasing is a way of leveraging and anytime you can use another person's money (as in the property owner), you should do so. Basically, there are five ways to lease:

The Straight or "Flat" Lease.

This is the basis of all lease types and the oldest form of leasing. It simply sets a single price for a definitive period of time. It is the best deal you can get for three to five years. It will state that you have full access to the leased property and are liable for the contents and the premises. It may or may not give you the right to re-new the lease at the end of your term, and you need that provision. It is not a good idea to have a flat lease for too short a period of time, like one year. A series of short term flat leases will cost you more than a long term lease with favorable escalation clauses.

Net, net-net and triple net leases.

There are three things that affect your lease cost: insurance, repairs and taxes. Variations of these items are reflected in the actual cost of the lease space plus one or a combination. Therefore a net lease may state that you are responsible for one of the items, so it would be the base lease cost plus building insurance for example. The net-net lease holds you responsible for two of the items, and the triple net lease states that you are responsible for all repairs, taxes and insurance. If you are a landlord and leasing space to a business person, you would love to have them sign a triple net lease.

Step lease

This lease will accommodate the landlord's expected increase in expenses by increasing the rent on an annual basis over the life of the lease. The problem with this type of lease is that anticipated expenses are based on estimates and not actual costs. There may be an adjustment clause, but it is rare. There is no way for either party to be sure in advance that the proposed increases are fair.

Cost of living lease.

This provision ties the annual increase in rent to the cost of living index rather than on anticipated expenses. Rent goes up with general inflation. Depending on the base rent, this type of lease can be very appealing especially if part of a net lease. Consider also that the prices of your products will increase with inflation.

Percentage lease.

As suggested, this lease is based on your sales, either a minimum amount, a base amount, or a percentage, which ever is higher. These percentages can be as high as 12 percent but are generally in the 3 percent range. Many times a percentage lease is combined with one of the other lease types. So you could have a flat lease or step lease with a percentage added at the end of every year. In effect this becomes a cost of living lease by adding a percentage of sales to the base amount. If the landlord insists on a pure percentage lease where he will not charge a monthly rent but take a percentage of sales every month then you will have to provide him with proof of sales and a financial statement from your CPA

Final tip: always remember that the landlord is writing the lease and it will always be in his favor. For example if you no longer need the leased location and you are one year into a three year lease, the lease will not let you just get up and leave with a nice letter to the landlord. You will be required to pay him the full lease price for the two years remaining. Or, if he is a nice person he may let you sub-let the property, but seldom will he let you go without a penalty. SO BE SURE YOU UNDERSTAND THE PROVISIONS OF THE LEASE AND THE PENALTIES.

Marketing Your Image

If you know what product or service you will be selling in your new business, and you fully understand your market, your competition and how you will appeal to customers in the market niche you have identified, then we are ready to start putting the parts together. Keep in mind that up to now we have concentrated on making sure there is a market for your product and who your customer will be. That is critical to the next step.

What's in a Name?

Plenty. When you select a name for your business it should tell what you do. Many business owners think "cute" is going to attract customers, it does not. If you are making and selling axe handles, do not call your business "Hickory Heaven," call it what it is: "Jones Axe Handle Company." By naming a business according to its product or service you are advertising without having to explain. You need to establish your "brand" in the minds of your customers so they associate what you offer with your name. Once established you can begin to abbreviate and become unique. Let's take Cracker Barrel as an example. When they first began it was "Cracker Barrel Restaurant and Old Country Store." Once they had established their brand they were able to simply say "Cracker Barrel" and people knew it was a great place to eat with a unique atmosphere. This is called conditioning the public. In starting your business you do not have that level of recognition, but your company image is as important to your success as a terrific product, great service and a solid business plan.

First impressions are made several ways and how you present your name is critical. Every time you hand out a business card, send a letter or advertise on radio, TV or in the newspaper you are promoting your name hoping people will remember. Even the look of your office, delivery vehicles, and employees conveys a message, and if it is a name that does not say what you do it will not imprint in the minds of potential customers. There is a tremendous demand for the attention of the buying public and people forget almost instantly. So, "Arlenes Angels" says nothing, but "Arlenes Cleaning Service," tells what you do. You can add the Angel part later on in your advertising.

Claim Your Name:

After you have decided on a name for your business it is important to make sure it does not belong to someone else. A simple call to the Secretary of State and you will find out, or in many cases your local business license office will have that information.

Think Professional, Be Professional

The first day you open your door for business you are a professional. You are going to bring value to your customers and provide a product or service that is so unique they cannot live without it. You are an expert and a consultant. You are the best that can be found in what you offer. With that in mind, just because you are a start-up company does not mean you have to look like one. Your logo, business card, stationary, brochures, signs and style are all part of a cohesive image program called **identity or branding**. With the right image your business can appear highly professional and give the impression of having been in business for years.

Here are some suggestions:

- If you have a home office be sure to have a separate telephone line for the business. Further more, be sure that telephone is answered professionally. The quickest way to say "I am not professional" is to allow a child or someone not connected with the business to answer with "Hello." sometimes with a TV or family noise in the background. The telephone MUST be answered every time with the name of the business and a name. For example: Ring, ring, "Good morning, Jones Axe Handle Company, Jones speaking." If you are out of the office have a telephone answering service take your calls, and insist that they answer the same way.

- Get your own web domain. If your email account still ends with @bellsouth.com, or @ roadrunner.com, some other ISP name, it's time to improve your image. Receiving customer communications through such an address is unprofessional. Get your own web site. I recommend www.sutherdyne.com as an inexpensive source for start-up businesses.

- If you cannot design an attractive web page have someone do it for you, then tie your email account to reflect @ your company name.com. DavidJones@Axehandle.com looks better than DaveandShirley@aol.com. Your current ISP may make this change for you. It could cost a little more but is worth it, and can be written off as an expense.

- If you have a home office it is often difficult to arrange customer meetings. Inviting customers to your home will not reinforce your image. Instead, use the conference facilities at your local library, or find a business conference site where you pay by the hour. Of course, meeting at a restaurant for lunch is always a good choice.

- Do not print letterheads or brochures on your printer. This screams: "I'm new and just getting started." Either design a logo or have a graphic artist do it for you. Remember, the simpler the better. Do not design a complicated four color logo when a clean two color design will do the job. Make sure your business cards, stationary, brochures, invoices and any other printed material you use uniformly have your logo, web address, and company name, address and telephone number. Have these things printed on a good quality paper by your local print shop. Your graphic artist can probably arrange this for you in a package deal.

- If you have a delivery vehicle make sure it is properly identified with your company name address and logo. If you use your personal car in making customer calls or even making deliveries, you can get an attractive magnetic sign to attach to the doors. Here you need a word of caution. Be sure your auto insurance covers you for business trips. Check with your insurance agent, and if business trips or alternate drivers are not covered, a simple "amendment" to your policy can be put in force.

Chapter Six Summary Questions.

1. What is the most important factor in starting a new business?
2. Where do you find trade associations for your business?
3. List at least three other sources for information that will help define your customer.
4. How do you get information about your competition?
5. Define "Market Niche."
6. What steps should you follow to find the right location for your business?
7. List the things you need to do to create your professional image.

Assignment: Go to your local public library and ask for the "Encyclopedia of Trade Associations." List at least two for your business. Call them and ask about membership. What did you find out?

Chapter Seven

Promoting and Selling Your Product or Service

It is important to make this point perfectly clear: In a start-up business the one thing you are selling is yourself. It is an interesting fact that your banker, vendors, and yes, even your customers, are not thinking about your business or product. They are evaluating YOU. If your banker loans you money to start the business *you are the one who has to personally guarantee the loan*–not the business. It is your credibility that gets the loan. We talked earlier about making sure your credit score is good. The business you are starting has no track record. The banker does not know if it is going to be successful or not. Your suppliers, or vendors, will ask you to fill out a credit application and because you have no other suppliers to put down as references they will depend on your personal credit history and your credit score. After your business has been successfully operating for two or three years they will begin to consider your business as a responsible entity. With all that in mind, the burden is totally yours to present yourself to your advisors, lenders, vendors and customers in a way that gives them confidence in you and makes them want to do business with you.

Pricing Your Product or Service

Pricing is a function of marketing because you need to be competitive and still make a profit. The nuts and bolts of how you price is based on your break-even figure and the profit you can live with. Breakeven is covered in Chapter Nine. Meanwhile, there are some marketing rules for pricing that you need to know.

Setting a realistic price is a daunting task. You don't arrive at it simply by whim or thinking it is fair or unfair. It is an exact science. So if you did not have a class in pricing in college, then use these five rules as a beginning once you know your breakeven point.

1. Never set your price lower than what it costs to stay in business.
2. Bigger things are always more valued than smaller ones. That is probably why software manufacturers package small disks in big boxes.
3. It is always easier to substantially increase your prices when you have fewer competitors (airline seats for example) than if you have a lot of them (like gas stations).
4. If you have a service business and you want to charge high prices, don't be afraid to start on the low end of the scale (just above breakeven) and raise your prices later on. But first, develop a reputation for exceptional service.
5. If you have to increase your prices shortly after starting your business, consider offering something that will make the product or service more valuable; changing the packaging or adding more support to your service.

It Comes Down to Selling

Let us assume that your product or service is something that a potential customer is already buying from your competitors. Your unique competitive edge is that you can do it better, faster and with a better guarantee. Your customer may have been buying this product from your competitor for several years, so why should they change? It comes down to SELLING. Remember, in the first chapter I said that the ability to sell is critical? And if you don't enjoy selling maybe you should think about not starting a business? It is YOU they are going to buy from. The fact that your product is somehow better has to be proved. Your customers are already happy with your competitor's product, so why change? Because, you have SOLD them on your credibility and professionalism and they feel comfortable doing business with you

That is what selling is all about. Think for a moment about business people from whom you buy things. Besides convenience and location do you find yourself going to the same teller at the bank; the same cashier at the grocery store; the same dry cleaner? Why? Because like the rest of us you feel comfortable doing business with certain people. It is that comfort level you have to establish with your customers.

Insurance companies have known this for ages, and they have intensive training programs that teach their agents how to establish that comfort and credibility level with potential clients. They know how to put you at ease; establish a personal connection and establish themselves as experts that have your personal interest at heart.

Selling is the end result of marketing. Everything you have done in researching your market, identifying your market niche, and determining your competitive edge finally comes down to presenting your product to a prospect in that market. They are not going to come to you just because you have advertised, and even if they do you are still going to have to sell yourself to them.

The Story of a Salesman

Howard Vansant was a paper products salesman who called on print shops. Printers use tons of paper and there is a lot of competition for their business. I had several print and copy shops at the time and I was satisfied with the quality, delivery service and selection being provided by the two large paper suppliers I had been buying from for years. All we had to do was call in an order and it would be delivered, often the same day. So, I never thought about changing as I had no problems with this end of my business. Then one day a paper salesman from a new paper company introduced himself to me. He simply said "I'm Howard VanZant with Walters Paper Company and if there is ever anything we can do for you just call me." He handed me his card and left. I tossed his card in the basket and thought no more about it until one week later Howard appeared again and announced that they were having a special price on a popular type of paper. Again I said "Thanks but no thanks" and Howard left. The next week, the same day, Howard appeared again, this time with a catalog of all the types of paper they carried in their warehouse and another business card. I said "Thanks." It was a well prepared catalog so I put it in our catalog file with the other paper companies. He would always ask, "Is there anything I can do for you today?" and again I said no. It started to dawn on me that I never saw a representative from the paper companies I was buying from, and here was Howard every week asking what he could do for me. The fifth time Howard stopped by it so happened we had just run out of a certain type of paper we needed to complete an order. Because he was standing there I said "Do you have this paper and how soon can you get it here?" Without hesitation he said they had it in stock and he would go get it personally and bring it right back. When he returned with the paper he asked if he could go through our warehouse stock to see if we were running short on any of the other fast moving items. He did and came back to me with a list of paper items that we needed saying I can have these for you in the morning. He got the order, and many orders after that. He showed me he cared about my business and was willing to go that extra mile. It was a long time before his competition found out what Howard's secret was and by then he had captured many of the large printing businesses in town. He established himself as a credible person who was willing to personally service an account.

How Persistent Should Sales Calls Be?

- 80% of all sales are made after the fifth call, but...
- 48% of salespeople call once and give up   (on the first call the prospect forgets)

- 25% call twice and quit   (on the second call they might listen)
- 12% make three calls and stop   (on the third call they might remember)
- 10% keep on calling   (on the fourth call they think)
- It is this 10% that make 80% of the sales   (on the fifth call they buy)

Why do Customers Leave You?

- 1% Die
- 9% Competition gets them
- 14% Unhappy with service
- **76% Quit because of your attitude toward them.**

Advertising and Promotion

Advertising and promotion of your business is an important part of your marketing program. First you need to get the most exposure for your money. Let's assume you have established a budget for advertising based on your anticipated sales. Your opening day promotion should not use up the budget you have estimated for the entire year. So, our guideline in this chapter is *"getting the most bang for the buck."*

Knowing where your customers are.

Once you know your target customers you will have to reach them. Advertising and promotion can be very expensive, and one of the reasons we discussed market niche was to formulate an advertising plan. Keep one thing in mind, you cannot compete with companies who buy TV time during the Super Bowl or advertise in Time Magazine. Ads like those would not be effective for you anyway. You will succeed in reaching your customer by being very selective and not by trying to be all things to all people. Remember when I asked you to identify your customer earlier by age, location, income, interests buying habits? That market segmentation gives you the information you will need to guide you to the right media. For example if you are starting a business selling garden tools nationwide by mail order, it makes sense to advertise on the internet, or in national magazines that cater to gardeners, rather than in the Wall Street Journal. However, if you are selling garden tools from a store in your neighborhood, your customers will be from the local area and it makes more sense to advertise in newspapers, local magazines or maybe commercials on local radio and TV.

What Media Should I Use?

This is a big question, and the short answer is: use the media that gives you the most for your dollar. Considering the fact that your advertising is on a budget and you probably do not have a lot of excess money to spend, your selection is limited. First of all, advertising is very expensive and while you may think that everyone who subscribes to a newspaper will read your small ad, very few actually will. So let's take a realistic look at your options:

Newspaper:

The cost of display ads are determined by population and the number of subscribers. People who sell advertising for newspapers like to say, "We have 150,000 subscribers, therefore that many people will see your ad." The truth is maybe 1% will actually see it. Potential buyers tend to look for ads in their immediate area of interest. A person interested in buying a lawn mower will not study an ad for tires. The cost of a two column by 6 inch display ad in an average newspaper is determined by their cost per inch formula, and will typically be about $600.00 for a one time placement. If you want the ad is a specific part of the paper, such as sports, or travel section, it will cost even more. So what do you have? You have spent $600.00 for an ad that few people will read, and it is in the trash the next day. The conclusion: this is a bad deal for a start-up business. Later on, when your business is successful, you may decide to run a special with a discount of some kind, and you can afford to run the ad for several days in a row. The repetition of the ad and the discount perhaps will create sales.

Magazines and Catalogs:

The same logic applies to these publications as it does to newspapers. They are expensive and not for start-up businesses. The advantage they have over newspapers is longer shelf life. Look in any doctor's waiting room and you will find magazines that have been there for years. The exception to the rule here is found in highly specialized magazines. For example, if you are selling karate uniforms and supplies, you can effectively advertise in one of the many karate publications found on magazine racks with good results.

Radio and Television:

Expense and repetition is still the rule. A 30 second ad on the radio can cost $150.00 and the same time on TV will likely cost twice that amount. The cost is based on the number on listeners the station claims to have and this is determined by surveys the stations pay to have done. Both of these media like to sell "packages" of air time that can range from a certain number per month or per year. Buying a package can get you a reduced rate on the per second cost. Unless you are buying a franchise where advertising is subsidized, both radio and TV are too expensive for a start-up.

Let's say that you have an advertising budget based on a percentage of gross sales, and your projected monthly sales are $10,000. If you are setting aside 10% for advertising and promotion, you have $1,000.00 to spend. This can give you two ads in the newspaper or possibly five 30 second radio spots. This will not create sales.

Bill boards:

This is probably the least effective way to advertise. First, no one reads them, (try to remember a billboard you saw last week), and second, they are very expensive. Here again, you need lots of exposure. Billboard companies sell packages of "saturation" where 50% would mean half of all the billboards they have in an area. This is very expensive and not a wise choice for a young or start-up business.

Yellow Pages:

For some reason every business owner seems to think that placement in the Yellow Pages is a requirement of doing business, like having business cards or a sign in front of your building. Certainly, the Yellow Page sales person wants you to think that way. Here again, think of the expense, and what you get. The ads are based on the number of directories they distribute in an area. So, the larger the metropolitan area, the more expensive the ad. A small one column by three inch ad can cost $250.00 per month, and you have to sign a one year contract. A small ad like that will be placed at the end of the listings because they are positioned according to size. The big full, or half page, ads are in the front. If a potential buyer is looking for the product or service you are selling they will see lots of ads before they get to yours.

Having your business listed in the Yellow Pages is a judgment call. Some business owners feel it is a necessary expense and devote their entire advertising budget to it. Others can run a successful business without it and use other forms of promotion more effectively. For example:

I conducted a survey in my six copy shops several years ago, asking customers how they found out about us and why they took the trouble to use our services. The survey included newspaper, radio, yellow pages and word of mouth. First, by a large margin, was word of mouth–other customers had recommended us. The last reason, with only ten votes out of 1200 responses, was the Yellow pages. As a result I discontinued my ad, and because I had a quarter page ad in the Printing section I saved over $14,000.00 per year. I took the money I was saving and hired a sales person with the same amount as a guarantee plus a commission, and my sales doubled within two years.

Direct Mail:

This is probably one of the most effective ways to let potential customers know you are ready and able to provide the exact service or product they need. If you have done your market research as we discussed earlier, then you have compiled a list of potential customers. DO NOT send them a bulk mail flyer. It will be thrown away. You should type a personal note about your business and how you can bring value to them, and send it with first class postage. Use your business letterhead and good quality stationery; address the envelope and the letter to a person, not to "resident" or "neighbor." Use yourself as an example. You may throw away a bulk mail piece addressed to "Resident" but you will open a first class letter addressed to you personally. My suggestion is that you select 50 of the names on your mailing list and take the time to print them, sign them in blue ink, and mail 50 different names per week. Don't try to do them all at once, because if you have a typical mailing list you will probably have over 1000 names. This tactic of personal, first class mailing will result in as high as 25% response. Keep in mind that the letter you send is telling them about your product and how it will bring either price or functional value to them. Earlier I mentioned that I would explain how to use mailing lists. If you took my suggestion and checked "Google" for "Mailing Lists" you found several services listed. (Yes, you can find them in the Yellow Pages too). The basic information that all of these companies use comes from Dun and Bradstreet and the U.S. Census Bureau. There are other data collection services that collect personal information. The mailing list companies buy that information and organize it to suit your purpose. For example, if you want a list of the names and addresses of Physicians who are under 35 years of age; have two or more children; like to ride bicycles and live in a house costing more that $350 thousand in a certain zip code, you can order that list. It will be guaranteed 90% accurate the day you buy it. The point is, these mailing list services can provide you with a potential list of customers to fit your specifications. The lists are expensive and can be in several formats, either on CD, peel off labels, or gum backed. They will also have a minimum number you have to buy. I have used these lists and prefer the CD version because I always personalized my mailings, and I could use the list several times before the CD was out of date.

What is Best for You?

A new business or a start-up simply cannot afford to invest money into advertising that will not bring in customers. Your resources are limited so you have to be creative and leverage the fact that you are new to your advantage. You will never have this opportunity again! Here are some proven ways that you can use to build your business; develop a customer base and gain a positive identity in your community. These suggestions are proven and highly effective, better yet they cost you nothing. Remember in previous chapters I said that "you must like to interact with people, enjoy the challenge of selling to be successful in business?" This is where that trait will work to your benefit.

Get an Article in the Newspaper About Your Business:

This is the first, and possibly only time, you will have an opportunity to get your name out to the public in a newspaper article, because you are new and you are newsworthy. More than that, an article about you and your business gives you credibility that an ad never will and you can count on immediate business. There is also the residual benefit that you get when you send reprints of your article to potential customers. The key to getting this done is it must be news and not a disguised ad. An editor will quickly spot the difference. My suggestion is that you find someone, maybe a reporter for the paper, and pay them to write a newsworthy article for you. You can also call the advertising department of your local newspaper and ask them for a "news kit" which will tell you exactly what they look for in an article. At this point you can either send the article with pictures to the paper, or you can stage a grand opening complete with ribbon cutting. Many charities welcome the opportunity to be involved in a grand opening because they like the exposure as well. On one occasion I called the American Cancer Society and told them I wanted to donate $500.00 which would be a ribbon of $5.00 bills, to be cut for my grand opening. They not only provided a local beauty queen to cut the ribbon, but called two city officials who participated in the event. The newspaper sent a reporter to get the story, which I had already written, and to take photographs. The next day they published a complete story with pictures of my grand opening and donation to the American Cancer Society. I sent reprints to customers and prospects as a direct mail piece. I also had one framed and hung in the waiting room. The total cost was the donation to a good cause. If I had purchased an ad the same size as the article it would have cost over $1500.00.

Get Published in a Neighborhood Newsletter or Trade Journal: News letter editors are always looking for articles of interest. Write on the subject of your industry or your specific expertise. Keep your articles to a single topic–don't try to cover the whole thing in one article. Your best areas are local papers, business journals that your customers use, city magazines, and trade publications. Again, if you are not comfortable writing news articles, pay a professional to do it for you. The long term benefits outweigh the small fee he or she will charge.

Get on Radio or Television:

Call your local station and explain that you are willing to be interviewed as an expert in your industry. Does this bother you? Remember, you are perceived as a professional in your industry by virtue of opening your business. Your customers expect you to be an expert. One interview can lift you from an unknown to known in a three minute interview; the credibility is unmatched. The best stations to call are local radio or TV for a talk show segment. Getting ready for your interview is important. The station may ask you for information about your specialty before the interview so the host will have something to go on. He or she will also ask for additional information just before you go on. You need to develop a story and practice before the show to be prepared.

Speak in Public:

Offer to give a talk about your industry and your place in it to business and civic groups in your area. This is a great way to get your message out. It is a mistake to be too specific or detailed in this venue, your idea is to make an impact on your audience. If you are a good presenter people will assume you are a professional in your industry and want to do business with you. If public speaking bothers you join a local chapter of Toastmasters.

Give a Seminar:

Prepare a strong 30 minute Power Point presentation that you can give at a moments notice, and let people know you are available. Your customer's place of business; trade association shows; the Public Library, or as a last resort you can rent a conference room at a local hotel, provide refreshments and send out invitations. In this case give at least an hour presentation. In any venue, be sure to follow up with a phone call, letter or both to those who attend.

Join a Networking Organization:

There are a number of good networking organizations and the best advice is to ask around to find one you like. They all love new members so you will be welcome. The main thing is to make sure they are able to provide good leads for you. So ask the president of a networking group how many leads they hand to each other each week. My preference is Business Network International. Mainly because I had a good experience with them and received many good business leads that resulted in long term customers that I probably would not have otherwise found. It is important that the group concentrates on finding business for its members, not simply mingle and exchange business cards. Chamber of Commerce functions are notorious for mingling and gabbing. A lot of time can be wasted in that situation with no business resulting.

Publish Your Own Newsletter:

After you have been in business for a year or so, or after you have a good customer base, give some thought to publishing your own newsletter. There are a number of graphics companies that will provide a prepared layout for you where all you have to do is write a few articles and insert them in the spaces. Your trade association will recommend one that will have an industry related format, or you can readily find one on the internet. Simply write the articles you want to include, take the layout to your local printer and tell them how many you want. Some printers who will also mail them for you. The idea of a newsletter is to stay in contact with your customers. I used newsletters for many years in my businesses and found them to be very effective. At one time I used a humorous format and actually had customers calling to find out when their newsletter would arrive because they enjoyed it so much. At the same time they were reading articles I had written about my business and how I could save them money and bring value to their business.

Chapter Seven Summary Questions.

1. How do you find who your customers are and where they are located?
2. What is the best way to reach them?
3. What are the main things you need to do in selling your product or service?
4. List five ways you can promote your business at no cost to you.
5. How will you get an article in the newspaper about your grand opening?

Assignment: (1) Call a networking club in your area and find out what they can do for you.
(2). Describe how you would use direct mail as a way to reach your customers.

Chapter Eight

The Nuts and Bolts of Getting Started

> "If it wasn't for all the darned government stuff you have to do, starting a business would be fun."
>
> Small Business Owner

It is true, there are a lot of things you have to do before you can open your doors, both for your own protection and to allow you to operate as a legitimate business. Let's take a look at the process, keeping in mind that this is the launching pad that puts you legally in business after you have completed all the other things we have discussed so far. In this chapter I will explain how select a name for your business, decide on the proper entity, get professional help, the legal things you have to do and finally how to manage the risks you face.

Like it or not there are certain rules and regulations that govern businesses, and the course of least resistance is to comply even though we hate to fill out government forms. Let's start at the beginning.

Get Your Name

Generally, the first thing you do once you decide that you want to go into business is to select a name. In Chapter Six we discussed the importance of getting a name that reflects the type of business you are in. It is important that you select a name that has not been taken. To do this, you call the County Clerk's office or the Register of Deeds office, or go in and see them. They will tell you if the name is available for use.. Or, if you are incorporating you can call the Secretary of State's office. Why is this important? First, you are going to spend a lot of money promoting your business name, and second, you do not want someone suing you for using a name they have already registered.

Get Your Business License

Depending on the dollar volume and type of business you have, you may need a business license. Assuming you have already registered your name the process is simple. You will pay a small fee to the Business License Office and be granted a license. The clerk will direct you to any other offices from which you may need special permits. You will also receive forms to file with the State Department of Revenue for your Sales Tax ID number. This enables you to buy supplies for your business and not pay sales tax. Caution here–do not use the tax number to buy personal or "business use" items. You cannot use it to buy things for the business, like signs, computers, mops, etc., only those things that you are going to resell If you plan to have employees it will also be necessary for you to obtain an Employee Identification Number. You can check with the IRS for more information at www.IRS.gov. or the Secretary of State at *www.sec-state.*(inse*rt* your state initials).*us*.

Check the Zoning

If you are running a business out of your home you will need to check with the County Clerk when you get your business license to make sure you are not in violation of some zoning ordinance. Some homeowner's associations restrict the level of business activity that can be conducted from a home, so be sure to check with them as well. I know a case where a person bought an old six bedroom house, spent a lot of money converting it to a day care for elderly people, only to find that it was zoned for "residential only" and could not be used commercially. She should have checked the definition of "residential" before she started.

Open a Commercial Bank Account

Your bank will require a tax ID number to open a commercial account for your business. It will also be necessary if you want your bank to accept credit cards from your customers.

Before you select a bank for your business check around for the best deal. Many banks require a minimum deposit. They may also assess fees if your account goes below a certain amount. Find a bank that does not have minimums or fees. However if you are borrowing money from a bank to start your business, they may require that you also have your checking account with them. If not, shop around for the best deal. I recommend that you select a small bank rather than a big one, because it gives you a chance to get to know the people in the bank and this can be important to you later on. Go in and meet the president or vice president and tell them you are starting a new business and plan to do business with them. Establish a good friendly relationship over time, and remember that when you need advice the banker's time is free, whereas you will pay an accountant or attorney.

To Incorporate or Not

When you go to the **Business License Office** to get your license and tad ID number they will ask you about your entity. They are not getting fresh, they simply want to know how you have structured your business. There are three ways: Sole Proprietorship, Corporation and Partnership.

First, let us look at **sole proprietorship**. This is a business that is owned and operated by one person. There are no legal requirements to establish one, and in most states if you are operating under a name other than our first full and last legal name you must register the business as a trade name with the Department of Revenue. As the owner of a sole proprietorship, you have complete control of the business. This form is well suited to a small start-up business. You don't have to consult with any partners or stockholders and you are free to respond quickly to your market. Since you make all of the decisions you don't have to share the profits with anyone.

Just as proprietorships are easy to open they are easy to close. There are fewer legal requirements and restrictions that with a corporation or partnership. If you choose, you can liquidate your assets, pay your bills and turn off the lights. You are out of business and on to something else.

If your business shows a loss for the first year or two, those losses can be deducted from other income you might have. This advantage is short lived however because the IRS says your business must make money three out of five years, otherwise it is considered a hobby not a business. Still, this deduction can give you a boost if you are starting your business on a part time basis and have a full time job.

The big disadvantage of a sole proprietorship is you have all the liability. That means you are personally responsible for all debts or lawsuits the business incurs. Your personal assets are at risk and your home and car might have to be sold to cover the debts or lawsuits.

Another disadvantage: it is almost impossible to raise money for a sole proprietorship. Banks and investors always insist on the protection of a corporate entity.

Partnerships can be formed if two or more people are going into business together. It is defined as co-ownership of a business for profit. In many respects it is like a sole proprietorship in that the partners can deduct losses against other personal income, and they share the liability of any debts or lawsuits. The advantage of a partnership is that partners should bring complimentary skills and resources to the business to enhance its success, and they should have good business sense. It is critical that a partnership agreement be written by a business attorney under the rules of the Uniform Partnership Act (UPA). The intent of this law is to settle problems between partners. For example if one partner dies and his ownership in the business goes to his wife who has no knowledge of the business, how will the remaining partner run the business. An agreement about issues like this in the beginning precludes bad feelings and lawsuits. DO NOT start a business with a partner unless a partnership agreement has been signed, even if he or she is a close relative or a dear friend. Then, make sure both of you understand the agreement.

Corporations, C and Sub-S

A corporation is similar to a person; it is an individual entity in the eyes of the law. So, when you incorporate your business you are actually creating an entity for whom you will work as an employee even though you may own all, or most of the stock shares. A corporation is a business structure that is separate from its own managers and owners.

The C corporation is a structure that is organized through the state in which the corporate papers are filed. You can file in just about any state but I recommend that you file in the state where the business is located. Use a local business attorney to file the papers, do not use an unknown person who has an 800 number and promises to do it for $65.00. You never know when you may need an attorney and he can also make sure your annual corporation minutes are filed and legal obligations are met. A C-Corp. is different than a proprietorship or partnership in that articles of incorporation are established and filed with the Secretary of State. Then capital stock is issued which individuals or other entities can purchase, making them share holders and owners of the company. The corporate entity provides an umbrella over the shareholders from liability. If the company is sued by someone or another business, the C-Corp. is liable and not the shareholders, directors, or employees. The C-Corp. has it's own needs and requirements which are separate from the people who formed it. Because the corporation is an individual it must fulfill legal obligations, pay taxes and make yearly reports to Federal and State agencies. When profits flow to the bottom line the Corp. pays income tax. Then the remaining profits are distributed to the stockholders as dividends and they are taxed again. So, the same income is actually taxed twice. A good feature of the C-Corp. is that the company can be sold or merged through the purchase of stock, and you can issue stock to bring capital into the company.

Sub-Chapter S Corporation.

This type of corporation was brought into existence to give small businesses an alternative to the C-Corporation. While all of the filing requirements and articles of incorporation are about the same as the C-Corp. the big break comes with taxes. The S-Corp. does not pay tax on income, instead the profits or losses flow directly to the shareholders. The shareholders can deduct any losses from their personal income at tax time. The S-Corp. has certain limitations however, and among those is the rule that it cannot be merged or purchased as a corporation, and the S-Corp. is limited to 35 shareholders, and they must be citizens of the U.S. Of course, these things are generally not on the mind of a new business owner anyway as he or she is primarily interested in the absence of liability. Later on the S-Corp. can be dissolved and replaced by a C Corporation. I recommend that any new business owner consult with a business attorney to determine the best way to go. Even though you are starting small the type of entity that is best for you may depend on how big you plan to get.

Limited Liability Company (LLC)

As in corporations, there are several types of LLCs. Basically this is a form of business structure that has been around for a long time but has only caught on as a workable alternative in the last ten or fifteen years. Like a corporation, it provides the benefits of limited personal liability without a number of restrictions. Like an S-Corp. any profits or losses are passed on to the owners of the LLC, who are referred to as "members." An LLC more closely resembles a partnership in structure, and the IRS treats LLCs as partnerships. However it is similar to a corporation in that stock is issued to the members. Where the structures differ is that an LLC can issue more than one class of stock; voting and non-voting, while corporations issue voting stock. In addition, while S-Corp's require all stockholders to be U.S. citizens, an LLC does not. In short, an LLC is a business structure that contains the tax advantages of a partnership with the liability protection of a corporation. It is generally easier and less expensive to set-up than a corporation which makes an LLC an attractive entity for a small business.

Sources of Business Advice

While your best friends are always willing to offer free advice, it is often well intentioned but ill advised. Once you have established a relationship with a bank, (I mean you are doing both personal and business banking with them), you should be on a first name basis with the people there. I always recommend making deposits personally so you can be identified with your business. The bank manager, vice president or president can be a valuable source of information for you, and as previously mentioned it is free. They will know attorneys, accountants and business consultants who can help you. The banker is in a position to refer you to an attorney to set up your corporate structure, and a CPA to do your financials and taxes. These three may be called on to work together on a problem you may encounter, so the fact that they know and trust each other will work in your favor.

Beyond these professionals, good sources of advice can be found with your trade association, vendors and business consultants. I do not recommend "business coaches" which is a recent phenomenon. If you have a specific problem in your business you can generally find a consultant who specializes in that area of expertise. This can range from the writing of your original business plan to assisting with a merger with another company. Consultants can also do an analysis of your overall performance and make recommendations to improve.

There is a lot of free information available from the Small Business Administration that you can readily access at www.sba.gov. You can also check with the Business Network provided by the SBA at www.business.gov. Both good reference sites. You will find a complete list of internet sites for specific business problems in Appendix A.

Chapter Eight Summary Questions.

1. Once you have established who your customers are and how you will reach them, what are the next important steps?
2. Why do you need a commercial bank account?
3. Why is it important to have a local business attorney?
4. Explain the difference between a sole proprietorship, C-Corporation, S-Corporation, partnership and an LLC.
5. List the sources of business advice you will use.

Assignment: GVisit the bank with whom you plan to do business and meet the manager. Ask him or her what you will need to set up a commercial account for your business.

Chapter Nine

Keeping Track of your Money and other Financial Stuff

We will start this chapter with a few definitions, mainly because as the owner of a small business you need to understand that accounting is the language of business. You will be working with bankers, accountants and trade associations who deal with business issues every day, so it is a good idea to speak the language they understand

All businesses have certain things in common: the tools they use to maintain their books in order to keep track of sales and expenses and pay their taxes. It is essential in any business that records are maintained and sales and expenses are recorded. In this chapter you will learn how to maintain a paper trail and to record the financial activities of your business.

The Start-up Budget

How much money will it take to get your business started? You will need to list all of the items that are required to open the doors. The items I have listed here may not include everything you will need as you may have requirements unique to your business, but this gives you an idea of the process.

1. Initial rent and security deposit
2. Improvements and decorating
3. Office equipment
4. Equipment leases (like copy machines)
5. Telephone and fax installation
6. Office supplies
7. Inventory
8. Licenses and permits

9.   Insurance
10. Professional fees
11. Advertising
12. Stationery
13. Miscellaneous (usually 10% of the above total).

All of these expenses, plus those you may have added to the list, will get your business open. Notice I have added a miscellaneous item that is 10% of the total. It is a certainty that you will forget some things and miss your estimate by at least that amount. The best way to get accurate figures for this budget is to call the supplier who will be providing the item and get a quote. It is not a good idea to guess. You will also notice that I have not included salaries or wages. This is because they will be a part of your sales and operating budget which I will discuss next.. Also, you should have a **personal budget** that includes savings or income from a regular job that you will use until the new business gets started. If you plan to quit your regular job to start a business you will need enough money to live on until the business starts turning a profit. Therefore it is a good idea to create a personal budget to see how much you will have to have in savings until that happens. Generally you will need enough money for one year. So, it's a good idea to plan ahead and budget your personal expenses.

Sales and Operating Budget

Now that you have an idea of how much money it will take to open the doors of your business, you need to estimate what you think your sales will be and how much it will cost to operate your business on a monthly basis. This is covered in Chapter 10 in detail, but it needs to be addressed here as a part of your understanding of what you think your sales and expenses will be. Your banker will be interested in these estimates also. Here is an example of a typical operating budget for one month. You will need to project these figures for 12 months or more in your business plan.

Month
Sales $_____
-Cost of sales (1)   _____
=Gross Profit   _____
-Expenses (2)   _____
    Salaries   _____
    Rent   _____
    Utilities   _____

Telephone   _____
Advertising   _____
Insurance   _____
Postage   _____
Licenses & Fees   _____
Office supplies   _____
Interest on Loan   _____
Miscellaneous   _____
TOTAL EXPENSES   _____
-Taxes   _____
-Loan payment   _____
NET PROFIT AFTER TAXES   _____

(1) **Cost of sales:** this includes anything you buy to resell in your business. For example, if you are a florist, all of the flowers you buy from the wholesaler are cost of sales. Subtract this from total sales to get Gross Profit.

(2) **Expenses** are all those things you need to keep the business running.

Starting the Paper Trail

This term refers to the records that are maintained from the day you spend the first dollar in starting your business to the day you retire or sell the business. "Keeping the books" is the common denominator in all businesses. It means maintaining a solid financial record of every business transaction regardless of size; a ten cent copy at a copy shop or a thousand dollar purchase of inventory. A basic necessity in any well run business is to know exactly where you stand financially at any given time. Keeping good records is more a matter of developing good business habits than anything else. It will require discipline before it becomes an automatic practice.

I recommend that you start with a simple set of journals; one for expenses; one for daily sales and a monthly summary of all sales and expenses. I know there is an abundance of bookkeeping software programs available, but in the beginning you need to stay with the pencil and paper method. Why? because it is important for you to get the feel of posting to your journals and ledger sheets. There is no better way for you to understand the numbers in your business. Later on you can consider a software program like Quick Books and adapt it to your business. It is much better to make the computer program do what you need it to do through your experience in keeping your own books instead of trying to make your business fit the demands of the software in the beginning.

In getting started it is important that you understand that every cent you spend and every sale you make in your business needs to be recorded. At the same time DO NOT mix your personal expenses with business expenses. Every time you spend something for your business **get a receipt.** If it is for something for which no receipt is given, then make an entry in your journal showing the date, what it is for and the amount. There is an old saying in business "take care of the pennies and the dollars will take care of themselves."

Here are some of the things you will want your bookkeeping system to provide on a daily basis;
1. Available cash on hand (both in the bank and in petty cash)
2. Balance in your commercial bank account.
3. Record of all sales and cash receipts.
4. Total in accounts receivable (the amount customers owe you)
5. Total in accounts payable (what you owe suppliers).
6. Any debts you owe that are due in total or in payments.

Make sure at the close of every business day that all transactions are posted from your journal to your ledger and that the day is closed out. Petty cash is counted, deposits are ready to be made and all the items listed above are complete. It is hard to catch up and remember things if you get a day or two behind so "let every day take care of itself." Why is this so important? because it keeps you on top of your business. Whenever I hear someone say "the business is running me, I am not running my business," I know that they have fallen behind in keeping their records. Posting to your daily journals makes it easier to make entries in your ledger, and this in turn makes it easy to post to your monthly sales and expense ledger, and finally to your year-end sheets for your CPA. She will love you if you bring her neatly done monthly and yearly summary sheets. The worst thing and the most expensive is to bring her a box of receipts, deposit slips and sales records for her to sort through.

Journals and Ledgers

I mentioned before that your job is not to spend time in preparing financial statements; your CPA does that, your job is to run the business and sell your product or service. I discuss financial terminology only to familiarize you with the language of business, not to make you an accountant. However, your CPA does have to receive something from you that tells how you are doing, and that will be in the form of journals and ledgers which you will prepare. Your CPA will take the sales, cost of sales and expense figures from your ledger and prepare your financial statements and tax returns. Your job is to make sure they tell the whole story. You will maintain a daily **journal**, which is a chronological record of all the financial transactions you transact; things you buy for the business and things you sell. A **ledger** reflects a summary of your journal entries and separates them into accounts. Your journal will be by date and item. Here is an example for a men's clothing store, one day, July 15.

Expenses

Date:	Vendor	Reason	Amount	Receipt
July 15	Exxon Station	Delivery	$15.00	Yes
	Office Depot	Paper for copier	12.00	Yes
	City Newspaper		Advertising	150.00

Invoice

Total for the day   177.00

This information would be transferred to a specific account in the ledger. (Your CPA will give you a chart of account numbers to use.)

Account	Account #	Total
Delivery	2215	$ 15.00
Office Expense	2240	12.00
Advertising	2250	150.00
Income	4310	410.00

This becomes the basis for the financial statements your CPA will do for you. Your job is simply to record them as we have discussed. She will also set up your accounting system on an accrual or a cash method. The **accrual basis** is a method of accounting in which income and expenses are recorded *at the time they are incurred* rather that when they are paid. The **cash basis** is a method in which income and expenses are recorded *at the time they are paid,* rather than when they are incurred. The cash basis is the simplest to use and is generally appropriate for a very small business.

Every financial transaction in your business must be recorded in some way. Get into a habit of writing a receipt for every sale and recording every cent you spend in expenses. The cost of this course or this book is an expense to your business and can be documented as "training or education." Receipts should be kept in a file; the large expenses are filed by the date they are incurred, and the small expenses can be filed under "miscellaneous" and totaled at the end of the month. As mentioned previously, do not mix business expenses and personal expenses. Do not take ten dollars out of your business cash to buy your lunch unless you record the act as "salary to the owner." In the same way, do not write checks from the business for personal things unless they are recorded that way. Keep in mind that your business is a separate entity–it is like a person and you would not steal from that person.

Your CPA will take the monthly ledger of expenses and income and prepare three things: an income statement, a balance sheet and a cash flow statement. These are like report cards that show how well you are doing.

What is a Financial Statement? Simply stated, it is a written record of the financial status of an individual or a business. It consists of a Balance Sheet, an Income Statement, (sometimes called a Profit and Loss statement, or Operating Statement), and may also include a Statement of Cash Flows and a Statement of Retained Earnings.

A financial statement is called "*Common Size*" if percentages are shown for each line on the statement. Most statements prepared by CPAs will show these percentages. This is important to you when you want to compare the performance of your own business, to the industry standards provided by your trade association.

The **income statement** shows the revenue and expenses that are used to calculate the profit or loss for the month. The **balance sheet** is a financial statement which shows the total of your business assets (everything you own); the total of the business liabilities (everything you owe), and how much **equity** you have in the business after the liabilities are subtracted from the assets. The **cash flow statement** simply shows all the cash inflow (all the money the business can put together at a given time) and all the cash outflows (all the money the company is obligated to spend at a given time). The end result is how much money the business has available. The cash flow statement is a combination of figures from the income statement and the balance sheet and is the most important of the three in making decisions for the business. Here are some examples:

Income Statement (Profit & Loss for month of July)

Sales	$35000.00
- **Cost of sales** (things you bought to resell)*	12000.00
Gross Margin	23000.00
- **Expenses**	
Advertising	1200.00
Salaries	2400.00
Supplies	1800.00
Insurance	1500.00
Utilities	400.00
Miscellaneous	200.00
Payment on note	500.00
Other Expenses	350.00
Taxes paid	1000.00
Total Expenses	10350.00
Profit or(Loss)	12650.00

(All of these figures are taken from the journals and ledgers that you have maintained for your daily activity)

Balance Sheet
  Current Assets
        Cash in Bank $4000.00
        Accounts Receivable   2500.00
        Inventory   12000.00
        Supplies   350.00
        Pre-paid expenses 200.00
                Total Current Assets $19,050
  Fixed Assets *
        Real estate   50000.00
        Equipment   16000.00
        Lease Improvements   4500.00
        Vehicles   15000.00
                Total Fixed Assets $85500.00
  Other Assets
        Licenses   200.00
        Deposits   350.00
                TOTAL ASSETS $105100.00
  Current Liabilities
        Accounts Payable   3500.00
        Notes Payable (now)   1500.00
        Accrued expenses   350.00
        Taxes owed (now)   1000.00
        Total current liabilities $6350.00
  Long Term Liabilities
        Note payable in one year   25000.00
        Bank loans   50000.00
                TOTAL LIABILITIES $81350.00
                NET WORTH (assets minus liabilities)
23750.00
                TOTAL LIABILITIES & NET WORTH
$105100.00
    * Depreciation is not shown in this statement.

Cash Flow Statement

	Opening cash balance (from Balance sheet)	$4000.00
+	**Accounts Receivable** (collected this month)	1000.00
+	**New loans** (1 year note from bank)	25000.00
=	**Total** (money available right now)	39000.00
	Deduct: (every thing due right now)	
	- Expenses (from Income Statement)	10350.00
	- Accounts Payable (due right now)	3500.00
	- Notes due now	1500.00
	- Taxes due now	1000.00
	- Other expenses due	350.00
	Total Disbursements	16700.00
	Closing Cash Balance	22300.00

Depreciation on equipment and buildings would be added in to the total money available now because it is shown as an expense on the income statement, but is not money that is actually spent.

Throughout this book I mention **trade associations** as a great source of information. This is especially true for financial statements. Your trade association should be able to provide you with a full set of compiled reports representing region, district or national financials. These will be "common size" for easy comparison, so it is important that your CPA provides the same for your business.

When I owned a printing and copying business I joined the National Association of Printers and Lithographers. This trade association provided its members with regional financials; a compilation of all the member businesses in a given region. Mine was the Southeast, which included ten states and over 500 printing operations. The financials were broken down into shops in operation less than 5 years; then 6 to 10 years and finally 11 years or more. This breakdown recognized that each of these categories had a different set of problems and gave us an opportunity to compare our performance with others at the same experience level. I could look at my cost of sales, advertising or any other item on my Income Statement and see how I compared. If I knew my sales were down and saw that my advertising expense was also low, it suggested that I needed to spend more in advertising and promotion to bring my sales up.

Using Ratios in Your Business

I introduced and explained the "current ratio" in Chapter Five as a vital ratio in business, because it tells you if the business has enough assets to pay off its liabilities To find it, you simply look at the balance sheet and take the total current assets figure and divide it by the total current liability figure.

Current ratio = current assets ÷ current liabilities

Another more critical ratio of strictly having the cash to pay off liabilities is called the "Quick Ratio" and for this you use the following simple formula:

Quick ratio = Current assets – Inventory & Receivables ÷ Current Liabilities.

In this, you are saying that it may take time to sell off the inventory and collect the receivables, besides these items may be overstated, so let's just see if the cash in the business can pay off the liabilities. If it can, the business is in good shape. If not, then it will take the sale of these other assets to liquidate.

Then there are some important ratios that are called "**Activity ratios**." They show how the business is performing in the areas of Inventory, Accounts Receivable, and Sales compared to Assets. Yes, you need to know if the assets, like machinery, vehicles, and equipment are producing the sales they were purchased to produce. You can use either the "fixed assets" or "total assets." In this case we will look at the Total Assets of the business:

Total Asset Turnover = Sales ÷ Total Assets

This ratio measures how efficiently the business uses all of its assets to generate sales, so a high ratio generally reflects good overall management. A low ratio may indicate flaws in overall strategy, poor marketing efforts or improper capital expenditures. (Equipment, machinery, etc.).

We can do the same thing with Inventory. If you are looking at a business that has inventory you should want to know how fast it is turning over, that is, how long it takes to sell it from the time the inventory is purchased. Like all ratios, the significance of this ratio depends on the industry you are in. Generally, the higher the inventory turnover, the more times the business is selling its inventory. A high ratio implies efficient inventory management.

Inventory Turnover = Cost of goods sold ÷ Inventory

The Cost of Goods Sold figure is found on your Income Statement and the Inventory figure is found on your Balance Sheet.

If the business sells products on credit terms it will have *accounts receivable.* This is money the customers owe the business. The question becomes: How long will you permit your customers to use your money? Generally, a business expects the customer to pay them in 30 days or less, and may even provide a discount as an incentive to pay in less time. But in the real world of business we find that customers do not pay on time, and if your credit policies are not clearly understood, the customer may take more than 30 days to pay. In this case a ratio you need to know is called *Average Collection Period,* or, the Accounts Receivable ratio.

Average Collection Period = Accounts Receivable ÷ Average Sales per Day

The Accounts Receivable figure is found in the Assets section of your balance sheet. The Average Sales per Day is simply the Total Sales figure, found on your Income Statement, divided by the number of days. If this is for a year, then you would divide the sales figure by 365 to get the average per day.

The average collection period is a measure of how long it takes a business to convert a credit sale in to cash, and it indicates the effectiveness of credit granting and collection policies. High average collection periods usually mean the business is not effective in getting their money from credit customers, and could be an indication of serious problems. We will discuss more about establishing credit policies later on.

The last ratios I am going to suggest as tools in evaluating a business are the *Profitability Ratios.* They are used to measure the ability of a business to turn sales into profits and to earn profits on assets. Also, profitability ratios give some insight into the kind of job management is doing.

The first is **Net Profit Margin.** This ratio measures the percentage of each sales dollar that become

profit after all expenses and taxes have been paid. As I mentioned, it is a measure of management efficiency. This margin must be compared to those in your industry to have any meaning, but generally a low figure indicates that expenses are too high relative to sales.

Net Profit Margin = Net Income ÷ Sales

Net Profit is generally the last figure on your Income Statement. The Sales figure is the top figure on the statement; or Total Sales. The margin is expressed in dollars or cents and shows how much after-tax profit the business generates for each dollar of sales.

The last ratio I recommend for business valuation is **Return on Assets,** which shows you how well a business is utilizing available assets, (all of those listed as Total Assets on your balance sheet). This is important if you are analyzing a business because a seller can inflate his assets to improve the balance sheet. This would result in a low ratio, which indicates poor utilization of assets and a caution sign for you. A high ratio is good by most industry standards.

Return on Assets = Net Profit After Taxes ÷ Total Assets

The resulting figure will be in dollars or cents and shows the after tax profit for each dollar of assets the business has at its disposal.

Compare with Similar Businesses

As previously mentioned, there are a lot of different ratios used in business. The ones I have described here are indicators of liquidity, leverage and profitability. The thing to keep in mind is that ratios by themselves tell us very little. For analysis purposes, ratios are useful only when compared with the ratios of similar businesses. Their effective use depends on your ability to identify problems that exist in a business and to change conditions that have caused the ratios to fall below the standards.

Where do you find the ratios for businesses like yours?

1. Trade Associations. Once you have found the trade association for your business, (Every library has a directory of Trade Associations). They will have a compilation of financial information for their members, including industry ratios.
2. Robert Morris Associates (RMA) publishes industry averages for 392 specific types of businesses, by Standard Industry Code (SIC).
3. Dun & Bradstreet has been collecting financial and demographic data from businesses for over fifty years. They have the largest data bank of information in the world.

Commercial Banks, Accounting firms and University Bureaus of business research are all sources of business financial information.

Break Even

Okay, one last thing before we move on to Chapter 10. It is important for you to know where your break even is. That is the point where your sales and expenses are equal. You are not profitable, but you aren't losing money either. This point is also referred to by some older business people as "The Nut" which they referenced during the day to identify that point in sales when they were even to their expenses that day. They knew exactly what it cost to run the business at any given time and what sales they needed to make a profit. You need to understand "the nut" in your business as well.

Simply stated, break even consists of three elements: sales, variable costs and fixed costs. **Variable costs** are those expense items over which you have control. Looking at the Income statement on a previous page you can see that advertising, supplies, miscellaneous and other expenses are items you can increase or decrease if you want to, while rent, salaries, and utilities are **fixed costs**, or items that are constant month after month and you cannot change them, (a possible exception is salaries). So, variable costs plus fixed costs equal total cost. Why is this important? If your sales are down and at or below your breakeven point you have to do something. You can either increase sales or cut your variable costs to remain competitive. If you have to reduce prices to increase sales then you must cut your variable expenses, and if you increase sales by putting more advertising and hiring more sales people your breakeven point increases.

Breakeven Chart

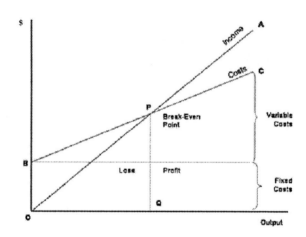

This is a simple chart showing where your breakeven occurs. It illustrates the impact of variable costs in your sales dollars. The bottom line (output) represents either dollar sales or units sold. The fixed costs are deducted from sales dollars on a constant basis (line B), where the variable costs increase with every unit or dollar of sales. The totals of variable and fixed costs are represented by line B-C, so where your total costs cross the income (sales) line O-A, your breakeven occurs. To make a profit in your business you obviously need to be past the breakeven point.

You can project your own breakeven point by drawing the horizontal output line and the vertical O-L line on graph paper. Then, project your sales in either dollars or units across the lower line in equal spacing using the squares on the graph paper. Next project your costs up the vertical line. Now take the sales figures from your projected income statement and mark where they will be on the lower line. Last, separate your variable from fixed expenses (costs) on your income statement as explained earlier; show where your fixed costs are on the vertical line, and plot where your variable costs will be with every dollar or unit of sales. This breakeven analysis is required in a business plan. And if you use the BizPlan Pro software referenced in the next chapter it will be done automatically for you.

Chapter 9 Summary Questions:

1. Explain why you need each of the following:
   A. Start-up (Sales and Operating) budget
   B. Personal budget
2. What are the components of a financial statement?
3. What is a "Common Size" statement?
4. Why are ratios important to you and when would you use them?
5. How would you determine the "Breakeven" for your business?

Assignment: Prepare the following for your business. (This will be required in your business plan).

1. Start-up budget
2. Income statement projected for three years.
3. Opening day balance sheet
4. Cash flow statement for three years.

Chapter Ten

Putting it all Together in a Business Plan

> *"A Business Plan is like a road map, you have a starting point and a destination with a definite time you will reach each stop along the way. It tells you how you will reach your ultimate goal."*

Putting Your Plan Together

If you have gotten this far and have assembled all the things we have discussed, you have most of the information needed to put together a good business plan. At this point let me make it clear that not all new businesses need a formal business plan. The purpose of a business plan is to attract money in the form of equity or a loan to start the business. Many start-ups have the money they need either from savings or cash flow from the new business itself. However, all new businesses need a plan of some sort regardless of what it is called; a strategic plan, a marketing plan, goals plan or objectives plan. The primary purpose is to establish your goals and how you plan to reach them. It is a road map and a time-line of where you plan to be at a certain time in the future.

Strategic Plan

Let us assume that you have the money you need to start your business, or your business is up and running, and you simply need a time line and a strategy of how you will reach your goals by certain dates, then a strategic plan of how you will reach these goals is all you need. Here is the five step process you will follow to develop your strategic plan:

1.   Write a **Mission Statement**. This provides direction for your business by answering the question: "what business am I really in?" The mission statement should be specific

enough to tell the reader something about your business and how it operates. It should not be a long, wordy document that explains the details of your business. Here is an example for a mop manufacturing company:

"To establish the Ajax Mop Company as the source of the finest mops in the world, while maintaining our uncompromising principles as we grow."
- *A great work environment where we treat each other with respect*
- *The highest standards of excellence in purchasing, manufacturing and sales.*
- *Develop great relationships with our customers*
- *Recognize that profitability is essential to our future success*

---

2. Write down what you consider to be the **Strengths, Weaknesses, Opportunities and Threats** of your business. (SWOT). Be honest, your gut feeling about these things helps you to establish goals to overcome weaknesses as you see them and to plan for perceived threats.

3. There are also **external** factors to consider. Write down what you think are the obstacles to achieving your mission. They are generally events or factors over which you have no control; a change in interest rates, a new government regulation or a competitor's new product. While you may not be able to control these threats you can prepare for them and put a plan in place to cope with them.

4. You have already analyzed your competition, so here is your opportunity to summarize your analysis. Without analysis competition can be viewed with bias. Your competition is never slow, backward and inferior as we would like to believe they are. Competition should always be given the respect they deserve. Take the analysis you have done and objectively identify the SWOT of your competition. The heart of your business strategy and the reason for your being in business is based on the weaknesses of your competition and the uniqueness of your product. You must do something better otherwise your business is not needed. Your competitive advantage must be sustainable over time.

5. In this step you begin to identify problems based on information you have identified so far. The process begins by drafting a list of alternatives; thus it is a two step process–identifying what is wrong and what you are going to do about it. It is primarily

based on your weaknesses and the strengths of your competition. The answer to these things becomes your goals, and the admission that something has to be done. While there is a strong temptation to list alternatives and strategies in your mind, it has been proven that getting ideas down on paper creates a wider range of options.

Goal setting and strategies. Your mission statement sets the broadest direction for your business. SWOT and competitive analysis help you refine and change direction. The goals you set must stem from your mission statement and they are needed before you can set realistic strategies. Your goals should be:

- *Written in terms of outcomes rather than actions*: A good goal states where you want to be, not how to get there. (Remember Chapter 2).
- *Measurable:* You must be able to tell if you accomplish your goal or not, so you must be able to measure the outcome you want to accomplish.
- *Challenging, yet attainable:* Goals that are too easy to accomplish are not motivating, so set a higher standard. "I will achieve $5,000. in sales by the sixth month," may be very attainable but not challenging. If extra effort and hard work can achieve $8,000. then make that your goal.
- *Communicate to everyone*: This is part of commitment. If you show your plan to your employees, attorney, banker, family and friends, there is an excellent chance you will not want to disappoint them. If you have employees, it is often a good idea to include them in the development of your strategic plan from the very beginning.
- *Written with a time frame for achievement:* Performance and motivation increase when people have goals with a time frame as compared to open-ended goals.

The Business Plan

The idea of writing a formal business plan as required by banks and investors is often viewed as a frightening chore. That is why there are professional business plan writers who will take the information you have assembled about your business and charge you a big fee to write a plan. I do not recommend this approach. First, it is your business and you should know every possible aspect of how it works. The worst scene you can imagine is sitting in front of a banker with a plan that was written by a third party, and being asked a question about which you have no idea because you did not do the research on that topic. So, before we get started in the process of writing the plan here are some rules:

1.   Do the research and the writing yourself. Spend the time in assembling the information we have discussed in this book. Be prepared for any question that an investor might ask.

2. Keep your business plan as short as possible. Big, wordy, lengthy plans do not impress anyone.

3. Keep the appearance of your plan simple but professional. Special bindings, covers, expensive paper and tabs are not impressive. The content is what the investors are interested in.

4. Do not hesitate to invest in some good software to help you write your plan. There is an impressive assortment of quality business plan programs available. My personal choice is **BizPlan Pro**, published by Palo Alto Software. It is available at any office supply store.

As previously stated, the purpose of a formal business plan is to **attract capital**. Most start-ups have to find money at some point and bankers or investors will typically ask, "Do you have a business Plan?" You have to understand the position of the banker. They are loaning you the money their depositors trust the bank to take care of. Therefore, the bankers are very conservative and they want the assurance that you are knowledgeable and realistic in your projections. Your business plan will show that you know what you are doing and have thought through the problems and opportunities. The other thing to understand is that bankers and investors will expect you to invest as well. Sweat equity counts very little. It is your hard cash they want to see in the business, often up to fifty percent of the money required to get the business going. Then, they will require you to collateralize all of the money they loan for your business. You say, "That's unfair, they want me to put up 50% of the money and still want me to collateralize the rest?" Remember, the banker is not going to risk one penny of his depositor's money. Can the SBA help? Yes, but the deal still has to go through the bank. The SBA guarantees only a portion of the bank's position in the loan. Angel investors are often times the best alternative to finding capital.

In addition to attracting capital your plan **provides direction** by showing how you will achieve your goals. Again, like a roadmap from point A to point B.

The business plan should prove that your goals are **attainable and feasible.** The very act of writing the plan is one of the best ways to prevent costly oversight. Committing your ideas to paper forces you to look critically at your means, goals and expectations.

If you choose not to buy software to help in writing your plan, there are many other good sources of information:

- Google–if you do a Google search on "Business Plans" you will be overwhelmed by the depth and magnitude of sources available.
- Small Business Administration–The SBA has a complete description of how to write a business plan along with tips and advice. www.SBA.gov then click on Business Plans.
- Your area Small Business Development Center will have plenty of free information, and perhaps classes in business plan writing.
- Community Colleges offer classes and free information.

Business Plan Contents

First, your business plan should be tailored to fit your particular business. Second, you need to consider your audience. Always keep in mind that big words, technical jargon and too much detail is often lost on an investor who has no idea of what these things mean. While a plan's content may vary from business to business, its structure is fairly standardized–therefore formal. Your plan needs to contain as many of the following sections as appropriate for your type of business.

Cover Page

Very simply, this page includes the name of the business, address, phone number, web address and the date the plan was issued. All of this is centered on the page as if you were addressing an envelope.

Table of Contents

You want the plan to be as easy to read as possible so give the reader an orderly reference to the major sections and the page numbers where they are found.

Executive Summary

This is a one or two page summary of your entire plan, and is usually written after the rest of the business plan is complete. It should briefly include four things: **What** the business is, in one short paragraph, including a description of your product or service. **Who** your customers are and how your product will add value to them (from your market research). **How** you will produce, or distribute your product, **Where** it will be done, and finally how much money you will need to accomplish these things. If you have an outstanding competitive edge that can be mentioned also.

Company and Industry

Here you need to describe the background of your company, your choice of legal entity and the reasons you started the business. How did your business get to the point at which it is today? Give a company history if appropriate and go into some detail describing what your business does and how it satisfies your customer's needs. Also describe the industry you operate within. Who are the major players and how long have they been in operation.

Products or Services

Once you have given the background of your company, you can go into detail describing your product or service. Again, try to avoid technical terms that may confuse the reader. A good idea is to write this section as if you were presenting it to a tenth grade student. Keep it simple. Describe how your product or service is different than those currently on the market and if there are any other uses that could increase sales. Include drawings or photos if appropriate. Describe any patents or trademarks that you hold since these give you a proprietary advantage. What is your potential for Growth, and what is your competitive advantage.

Market Research and Evaluation

There must be solid evidence that a market exists for your product or service. This cannot be something that you "think" or based on feelings or guesswork. Present the facts you have gathered on the size and nature of your markets. The banker will want to know if a large enough market exists and if you can be competitive. State the market size in dollars and units. Estimate your sales forecast based on your market research over a period of five years. That sales forecast will be the basis for projecting many of your financial statements.

- Identify your target markets and how you will reach them. (From your earlier market segmentation).
- Identify how you will continue to evaluate customer needs so you can improve your market lines and aid new product development.
- Identify your competition according to price leader, quality leader and service leader. Realistically discuss the strengths and weaknesses of each and how opportunity is created for you.
- Identify your market share. Since you have identified the size of your market and your competitors you can estimate the market share you intend to capture. It is often effective to use a pie chart to illustrate your point.

Marketing Plan

With the information provided in Market Research and Evaluation, you can now present your marketing plan. The idea is to show how you plan to reach your sales forecast, so start by explaining your overall marketing strategy by identifying your potential markets and deciding the best ways to reach them Your **marketing objectives** are what you want to achieve, and the strategies you will use to accomplish these objectives. For example, give a detailed description on how you will price your product or service, your break-even point and how you arrived at these figures. Then, how will you promote your product or service. What medium will you use to communicate the advantage of using your product or service to your customers? Then describe how you will sell and distribute your products. Will you have an in-house sales force, or use distributors? Tell how this program is structured so the reader will fully understand the process. Will you have service or warranty policies? Describe how it works.

Operations Plan

In this section you will stress elements related to facilities, location, space requirements, capital equipment, labor force, inventory control and purchasing. If you are starting a manufacturing business, outline the production processes and your control systems for inventory, purchasing and production. If you are in the service business then you should focus on location, overhead and labor productivity. Use these topics as a guide:

- **Geographic location**–Describe your planned location and its advantages and disadvantages in terms of labor cost, proximity to customers and suppliers, transportation available, tax rates, utility costs and zoning.
- **Facilities**–What kind of facilities does your business need? Discuss your requirements for floor space, parking, and special equipment. Do you plan to rent, lease or buy the space? How long will this space serve your needs and is expansion possible?
- **Control systems**–What is your approach to controlling quality, inventory and production? How will you measure your progress toward the goals you have set for your business?
- **Employees**–If you plan to have employees show how many you will need to start, then project your requirements over the next few years. Will you need to train them and can you do this and remain competitive?

Management Team

A successful management team unites people with complementary business knowledge, technical skills and life experiences. A great management team combined with a solid business idea and a proven sustainable market will always attract the capital to make their vision come true.

A venture capitalist once told me that a good management team with the right product is all he needed to make an investment. The importance of having capable experienced people on your team cannot be stressed enough. If that means just you and your wife or brother, make sure that the two of you have extensive experience in what ever role they will play in your business. The same goes if you are proposing three, four of five people on your team. There must be a good fit between the members of your team, the market you are entering, the opportunity your business will develop and the capability of each team member to make these things work. A knowledgeable investor will want a detailed description of the background and personal history of each person on your team, because if he or she is going to invest in your business they will want to know who is going to be spending their money, how it will be spent and how soon you will reach a positive cash flow.

The section of your business plan titled: **Management Team,** should first include a description of the job they will do then a detailed resume showing how their background fits the job. If you and a family member are starting a small business, then be sure to state what each of you will do and how your experience and background complements your responsibilities in the new business.

Tell how each member of your team will be compensated. Your chances of getting financing are very slim unless your team members are willing to accept a lot less than they might be paid by a big company while your business is getting started. You and your team members must show that you are committed to putting as many proceeds as possible back into the business.

It is also a good idea in this section to identify the outside advisors with whom you are working, including your banker, attorney, accountant, and insurance agent. Include their phone numbers and addresses.

Timeline

Show the timing and dates you plan to attain major goals. In addition to helping you calculate your business needs and minimize risk, the timeline is also an indicator to investors that you have researched potential problems and are aware of deadlines. A word of caution: people tend to underestimate the time needed to complete projects. Your time schedule should be realistic and attainable.

Risks and Assumptions.

This is an area that many business plans fail to include, and it is one of the most important to investors. They know that your business plan is based on hope and expectations, and they want you to tell them where the risks are in the business; the weaknesses in your business, and where you are assuming that things will happen. This section gives you an opportunity to state your alternate plans in case the unexpected happens. Here are some possible contingencies you should discuss:

- *Unreliable sales forecast*–What will you do if your market does not develop as quickly as you predicted? What can possibly cause a bottleneck in production, a dissatisfied customer or what happens if a key employee leaves?
- *Competitor's ability to underprice or make your product or service obsolete.*
- *Unfavorable trend in your industry.*

- *Trained workers not available as predicted.*
- *Your main supplier decides not to do business with you.*
- *Anything else you do not expect.*

Where are the weaknesses in your business? One of the first things an investor might ask is for you to identify where your weaknesses are. If you don't understand where you need to become stronger, then it is possible you do not understand the risks in your industry. Devote one page to the weaknesses in your plan and be able to explain them to an investor.

Financial Plan

This is where you show how all of the information in previous sections of your plan come together to form a viable, profitable business. One of the great features of the BizPlan Pro software is that the templates and format for the financials are automatic. You can bet that your banker or investor will spend a lot of time analyzing your financials so be sure they are accurate, realistic and complete.

Your projections are based on the performance of similar businesses in your industry; your estimate of how well you think you will do compared to similar businesses, and your analysis of the market you are in. Note: if your business is in operation then you will use historical (real) financials and pro-forma projections. Start ups will only have projections.

There are five financial statements you will need to include in your plan:

- Sources and uses of capital (initial and projected)
- Cash flow projections for three years (minimum)
- Balance sheets for three years
- Profit and loss statements for three years
- Breakeven analysis

There is more information on financial statements for existing businesses in chapter nine. In the business plan keep in mind that you need to show conclusions and important points based on your best estimates.

Sources and Uses of Funds

This simple form shows where your money is coming from and how you are spending it.

The Sources and Uses of Funds Worksheet

Sources of Funds:
  Debt:
  Term Loans $_____
  Refinancing of old debt   _____
  Lines of Credit: _____
      Line 1   _____
      Line 2   _____
  Mortgage   _____

  Equity
  Investments $_____   Total Sources $_____

Use of funds: $_____
  Property   _____
  Inventory   _____
  Equipment   _____
                       _____
                       _____

  Working capital   _____
  Cash reserve   _____
                                 Total Uses $_____

Balance Sheet

The balance sheet shows all the assets owned by your business and the liabilities, or what is owed against those assets. The difference between them is your equity in the business, or what the company has earned. This is also called capital. Bankers and investors will calculate some key ratios, as explained in Chapter nine to help determine the health of your business. You need to prepare balance sheets ending each of the first three years of operation.

Balance Sheet
(A balance sheet shows what you own and what you owe)

	Year 1	Year 2	Year 3
Current Assets			
Cash	$_____	$_____	$_____
Accounts Receivable	_____	_____	_____
Inventory	_____	_____	_____
Supplies	_____	_____	_____
Pre-paid expenses	_____	_____	_____
Fixed Assets			
Real Estate	_____	_____	_____
Equipment	_____	_____	_____
Leasehold Improvements	_____	_____	_____
Vehicles	_____	_____	_____
Other Assets			
Licenses	_____	_____	_____
Deposits	_____	_____	_____
TOTAL ASSETS	$_____	$_____	$_____
Current Liabilities			
Accounts payable	_____	_____	_____
Notes payable now	_____	_____	_____
Accured expenses	_____	_____	_____
Taxes owed	_____	_____	_____
Long term liabilities			
Notes payable after 1 yr.	_____	_____	_____
Bank loans	_____	_____	_____
TOTAL LIABILITIES	$_____	$_____	$_____
NET WORTH	$_____	$_____	$_____
(Assets minus liabilities)			

Cash Flow Worksheet

The most important financial statement for a small business is the **cash flow statement** because if you run out of cash you are out of business. This statement shows you that from your opening cash balance you add the money that comes into your business for a given period of time, (week, month, quarter), then you subtract all the money you spend for the same period. The result is your closing cash balance, which becomes your opening cash balance for the next period.

You should project a cash flow statement by month for the first year of operation, then by quarter for the second and third years. Cash flow shows you what the highest amount of working capital will be. This can be real critical if you sales are seasonal.

Cash Flow Work Sheet
   Sample Components of a Cash Flow Balance Sheet
   (A cash flow statement shows you how money enters and exits your business)

Opening cash balance
   Add: Cash receipts
      Accounts rec'ble
      New loans or investments
      Other sources of cash
         Total receipts

  Less: Utilities
      Office supplies
      Accounts payable
      Leased equipment
      Sales Expenses
      Loan payments
      General expenses
         Total disbursements
 Cash increase or
 (decrease)
 Closing cash balance

Profit and Loss Projection

Please be aware that your **profit and loss statement** will not be an accurate projection of the future. You are assuming (guessing) what your sales and expenses are going to be. There is no way to accurately determine your sales, cost of sales and expenses will be three years from now. That is why you use the industry figures from your trade association; to get an idea of what they might be based on historical figures. In making your projections, it is helpful to break sales down by product line or services and to determine the best-case scenario, a worst case and somewhere between these two extremes.

Start with the left column to show what your sales and expenses would be under the worst of conditions. In the right column enter figures that will appear if everything goes right, exceeding your expectations. The "Most Likely" figures will be somewhere in between. These three columns give a banker or investor an idea of your expectations and an opportunity to ask you why you have entered certain figures. Question and test your projections before you ever show them to anyone. Be prepared to answer hard questions about how you arrived at these conclusions.

Profit and Loss Projection
(Projecting the best and worst that could happen helps you calculate what your profits or losses are likely to be)

	Low	Most Likely	High
SALES			
Product or service	$_____	$_____	$_____
Cost of goods sold	_____	_____	_____
GROSS PROFIT	$_____	$_____	$_____
EXPENSES			
Variable			
Payroll	$_____	_____	_____
Commissions	_____	_____	_____
Delivery & Freight	_____	_____	_____
Travel & Entertainment	_____	_____	_____
Semi variable			
Advertising & promotion	_____	_____	_____
FICA & payroll tax	_____	_____	_____
Supplies	_____	_____	_____
Telephone	_____	_____	_____

Fixed expenses			
Rent	_____	_____	_____
Utilities	_____	_____	_____
Property taxes	_____	_____	_____
Professional fees	_____	_____	_____
Equipment leases	_____	_____	_____
TOTAL EXPENSES	$_____	$_____	$_____
Profit before depreciation	_____	_____	_____
Depreciation	_____	_____	_____
NET PROFIT or (LOSS)	$_____	$_____	$_____

Breakeven Analysis

You will have to show the reader how many units of your product or dollars worth of your service will have to be sold to cover your costs. A breakeven analysis will give you a sales projection needed to break even. It is the point at which you are neither making nor losing money. Here again, you need to compare your breakeven cost with similar businesses in your industry to be meaningful. It is a relatively simple formula as show below, using figures from your profit and loss statement.

Breakeven Analysis	Month 1	Month 2	Month 3	Month 4	Month 5
(At what point do you make money?)					

1. Total Sales
$_____
2. Fixed costs
_$_____
3. Gross Margin
$_____
4. Gross Margin as a % of sales

_____
   (Line 3 ÷ line 1)
5. Breakeven sales
$_____
   (Line 2 ÷ line 4)
6. Profit goal   —
$_____
7. Sales required to achieve
   profit goal
$_____
   (Line 2 + line 6 ÷ line 4)

Appendix to the Business Plan

If you have supplemental information that you feel is necessary to substantiate some of the claims or figures in your plan the Appendix is where you put them; Resumes of owners or key employees, advertising samples, an organization chart, financial statements and tax returns of the owners. Each item needs to have a separate appendix reference with letters of the alphabet (Appendix A, Organization chart; Appendix B, Resumes of Owners, Appendix C, Trade Association References, and so on).

The Total Job of Writing a Business Plan

Writing a business plan is a project that involves a long series of interrelated steps. Beginning with your idea for the business, you want to determine the feasibility through the creation of your business plan. Each step involves research and information that you can prove. It involves commitment to reaching goals and benchmarks that you have established in the plan, and the very last thing you do is to write the executive summary which puts all of the work you have done on one or two pages so the banker or lender can get an idea of what the following pages will prove to justify the money you are asking for.

Chapter 10 Summary Questions:

1. Explain the difference between a strategic plan, marketing plan, and a business plan.
2. Why is the mission statement so important to a strategic plan?
3. Why is the executive summary the last thing you write for a business plan?
4. Identify four sources of information that can help you with your business plan.
5. List the major sections of a business plan.

Assignment: Prepare a Profit and Loss projection for your business as described in this chapter.

Chapter Eleven

Step by Step Business Guide

Product or Service

Almost all businesses fall into one of these categories, however it would be difficult here to provide an outline of how to start all of the businesses that people want to start. One look at the SIC codes will tell you that there are thousands. However, there are some basic accepted rules for starting most businesses and that is what I have assembled here. The major categories are: Manufacturing, Service, Retail/Wholesale and e-Commerce.

I. **Manufacturing** is broken down into three sub-categories:
   A. Something that is fabricated or assembled, as in assembly line production.
   B. Food items that are prepared or processed, packaged and sold.
   C. Clothing items that are sewn in an assembly process

II. **Service** is considered any business that helps or adds value to an individual or a business.

III. **Retail and Wholesale** are businesses that purchase inventory from vendors, possibly processing in some way, then reselling to an end-user.

IV. **E-Commerce** is the newest addition to the business start-up scene, and one of the fastest growing. This involves business done on the Internet. As in anything worthwhile, starting a business takes thought and time, so be prepared to devote as much time as necessary to do it right. It is not a one day, one week or one month exercise, but an adventure that deserves your full attention and dedication until all of the facts are in and a written plan is in place.

The process of bringing your idea to the point of business readiness is critical to the ultimate success of your business, and the most important part of the process is to test the marketability of your product or service. The following outlines will give you an idea to the steps to be followed to take your idea from concept to the "ready to market "stage.

A.   Manufacturing—a fabricated or assembled Item:

Your idea is to manufacture, fabricate or assemble an item that will then be sold either directly to consumers, (as in direct mail, or through brokers), or wholesaled to stores or other manufacturers.

1. First, you need to make, or have someone make, a working model (prototype) of your item.

2. Prepare, or have prepared, a set of detailed drawings of your item. Be sure to date them and have a Notary Public witness your signature and date.

3. Contact a patent attorney and have her/him check your item for patent possibilities, and to make sure you are not infringing on an existing patent. If you can patent your item do so at this time. If your item is not eligible for a patent, and does not infringe on another patent you can still proceed with the idea, but with the knowledge that someone can also make and sell the same thing. Timing is important in this case. If the market test suggests that you have a great idea, then you need to act quickly. If you have selected a unique name or logo for your item we suggest that you have your patent attorney file for a registered copyright.

4. If you know a Company that is interested in manufacturing your item as a value added or adjunct item to something they are now doing, discuss it with them and you may work out a contractual arrangement with them that will be of benefit to you. If you have a patent on the item, they may want to buy it from you or give you royalties on it. Your own financial circumstances will be the best guide in this situation. However, if they want you to make it for their own use, then get a letter of "intent to purchase" with all the prices, deliveries and specifications agreed upon.

5. Now you have a critical decision to make. Should you: (1). Set up your own manufacturing facility or, (2) Have someone manufacture it for you. The first will take a lot of time and money in the tooling and assembly process. Plus you need to be very familiar with all the laws and regulations that govern this process. If you do not have the money to set it up, you may be eligible to apply for an SBA loan through your bank. Ask for the commercial loan officer who handles SBA loans.

6. Selection (2) may be the best way to get started. Be careful who you have manufacture your item; their time in business, reputation and ability to meet deadlines is critical.

Talk to a couple of their customers and learn more about them. You must have a good working relationship with them. Ask if they will give you terms based on your customer's "Letter of Intent". It is common for manufactures to ask for money up front, because you are new to them and the item they are making for you is new. So you still may have to borrow money to get the first order made. Also have your manufacturer sign a "non-compete agreement" which your attorney can prepare.

7. The sale and distribution of your item can be handled by you or by brokers. If you already have the contacts and they have agreed to buy your item, that's good. Otherwise you will need to contact brokers who already have the contacts. Go to the Business Reference Desk of your local library and ask them for the Directory of Registered Brokers, and select several Brokers who specialize in your product. When you call them make sure they do not handle a competitive line.

8. Liability insurance is important also, so check with your insurance agent for details. Theother things that you need to find out about are business licenses and permits. A call to your County Courthouse should answer these questions.

9. It is very important for you to know if you have the aptitude and personal skills to run your own business. Find out now by going to www. biztest.com, and select one or both of the skills and preparedness tests offered. This can be of tremendous benefit to you in your business.

B.   Manufacturing—food Item to be sold in stores.

We assume that you have successfully made this product, that it is unique in some way, and that you have been encouraged by family and friends to take the next step and make it in quantity for sale. The following steps will provide a guide to get you going:

A Market Test of your product is very important and there are several steps to be taken to get ready:

1. Carefully document (write down) the recipe or process involved in producing your product, take to a Notary Public and have them witness your signature and date on that document.

2. Select the container or package in which your product will be displayed in a store. Take your time and be sure you have exactly the container or package that best represents your product.

3. Your label is equally important because it is your "on shelf" sales tool. (a). First you will need a Uniform Product Code (UPC). If you are not familiar with this, go on-line and type www.upc.com. (b). Contact a graphic artist and have her design a label for you. (Do

not do this yourself unless you are really good and understand color separations and printing terms). (c). Your label will also have to list the ingredients and nutritional values of your product, so call the Food and Drug Administration in your state and ask for directions in doing this. Or, go on-line and type www.fda.gov. There will be instructions on what you need to do.

4. After you have accomplished the above, you will need to find a source to process or make your product. If it is a cooked product you will need a commercially rated kitchen. If it is simply a mix of dry ingredients, such as a cake mix, or the repackaging of already prepared items, check again, with the FDA for instructions.

5. Contact the Packaging Company again and have them recommend the proper packaging in which to ship your product. Try to get a package they already make otherwise it becomes very expensive.

6. Now you have the container or package for your product with appropriate labels, and the box in which they will be shipped. With this, make up several boxes that will be exactly as the stores will receive them. These are your sample boxes.

7. Now you are ready for the market test. Hopefully at this point you have spent less than $2,500.00 in getting ready. There are two ways to see if there is a market for your product: (1) Go to the Business Reference Desk of your local Library and get the names of first, a Product Research Company and second, Brokers who specialize in products like yours. Contact these people and arrange for them to market test your product, and for the broker to sell your product. Sometimes the broker can do both. Set a budget because market research can get expensive. (2) Take the product directly to the buyer of a chain store and present it to them. Unless you are really familiar this procedure we do not recommend that you try it. If you take your product to your friendly local grocer and have him put it on the shelf for a test, it will not tell you a thing about your product or its sales potential.

8. Once you have an idea of the market and a broker to sell your product, you will need a processing company to cook, mix or assemble, and package your product. We strongly recommend this approach for start-ups because it gives you an opportunity to check out the market and to see if sales will be large enough to justify doing your own processing and packaging.

C. Manufacturing—a clothing item.

Clothing items are one of the easier things to market test because of the nature of the industry. We are going to recommend ways for you to see if your idea has the potential for a good business.

1. It is first assumed that you are familiar with sewing, that you have a good sewing machine and that you have both designed and experimented with the item you have selected for a market test. This is not to imply that you are ultimately going to do the sewing of the item at home, only that you have the capability to make enough samples. You will need some photos of your item so have someone you know put the garment on and model it for a photographer. Get some real good shots from different views. We recommend that you hire a professional photographer for this because they know what to do.

    Take your photos, not the garment, and some of your business cards, (have some printed with your new company name, address and your name,) to the Clothing Merchandise Mart when they are having a trade show in a big city near you. Circulate and meet the buyers and brokers who will be there and show them your product to get their ideas. You may come away with some orders.

2. There are many clothing catalogs that will welcome new ideas. These direct mail services depend on new ideas like yours. Select the catalog that best represents the idea you have and contact them to find out what their requirements are for new items. they will want a photo of your garment and they will want to know how many you can produce. We will cover that in the next paragraph.

    If possible, it is not a bad idea to arrange to meet the catalog buyer and to personally take your sample and the photos to her.

3. In the event that you do get a large order for your item how will you produce them. Certainly not on one machine at home. And, it is not wise to buy other machines and hire people to do it, nor is it wise to sub-out the sewing to other people in their homes. You have no control over quality or schedules. The best thing to do at this stage is to find a company who is already set-up to sew on a production basis and to arrange with them to make your product.

    Have them sign a non-compete agreement and to give you prices to manufacturer your product. They will probably want a minimum order so be prepared.

4. Another suggestion, and one that has worked quite well for new idea garments, is doing the direct mail yourself. Select the one magazine that is best for your product. Contact their Advertising Manager, (listed in the front of the magazine), and ask what their requirements are for an ad and their prices. We suggest that you have a graphic artist prepare your ad for you. It is going to be costly anyway so it might as well be right! Go ahead and run your ad in the magazine, perhaps as many as three successive issues. You will get orders! and since the orders are coming directly to your home you can set your own production schedule for making, packaging and sending them to your mail order

customers. Finally, you can always do test market on E-Bay. Once you are signed on E-Bay and Pay-Pal, scan a picture of your garment; prepare a short description and price, then see what happens. One tip…be sure to acknowledge each and every order with a post card thanking them for the order and telling them about when their order will be shipped.

5. After you have tested the market for your product in one of these ways you may decide to begin the manufacturing process yourself. This both a costly and risky process and recommended only after you have established a large presence in the market. Until then let the processors (sub-contractors) do the manufacturing for you.

II.   A Service Business (that brings value to your customer)

A service business is one that assists, improves or adds value to another business or to a consumer. The service business can be operated from the owner's home or from an office/warehouse setting where supplies can be stored. For purposes of this explanation, we will not attempt to give examples of the hundreds of different services businesses except to say that the service business we refer to here does not require a retail location. If your idea is retail service oriented then you should go to the Retail Business page. If your idea involves the manufacturing of an item to be used in a service business then you need to go back to the Manufacturing page. In our reference, any service such as plumber, painter, window washer, graphic designer, drive-by oil change or courier service meets the service definition.

With that in mind, you have undoubtedly been thinking of turning your idea into a business for some time now. And, the steps to make it happen will be easy for you to do. Keep in mind that many fine service ideas have developed into very successful franchise programs.

We assume that you have progressed in the development of your idea to actually providing your service to someone and that this has been a successful experience. The next step is to turn this experience into a business. The following steps will show you how.

1. Before you go any further it is important to find out if anything like your idea is now being done as a business somewhere. Go to the national yellow pages on your computer and do some research. Then go to the Business Reference Desk of your local library and do some more research. We do not care if you find a similar business, competition is good for everyone, but you do need to know what is out there and how it is being done. Now, in the interest of certain legal things that may come up, make a detailed write-up of your idea, how it works, who your customers are and how you plan to service that market. Take this document to a Notary Public and have her witness your signature and date. Place the document in an envelope and seal it. then mail it to yourself. When it

comes back with the Post Office date stamp on it, do not open it. simply file it in a very safe place. This provides proof of your idea and protects you in case of questions later on.

2. It is important that you now test the market to see how well your idea sells. Be very selective, for example, if you have a dent removal service, go to a medium sized auto dealer and offer your service at a discount so you can build good will and have a reference.

3. If you need to hire people have them sign a non-compete agreement. Your attorney can prepare this for you.

4. Prepare a good-looking ad for the newspaper and run it no fewer than three times in the section that is appropriate for you. For example, if you have a wedding service you would run you ad in the Sunday bridal section. You can also run your ad in the trade publication that serves the industry you cater to. Do not advertise beyond your budget. 10% of your gross sales to begin with and 5% once your business builds up.

5. If your business becomes very successful you may consider franchising it to others..

III.   Retail Store or Wholesale Business

If your business idea involves opening a retail store requiring a storefront, or a wholesale business in which inventory storage is required, this is the section for you. We treat each of categories separately so choose which one best fits your idea:

(A) **Retail Business,** that requires that does not require a walk-in or drive-by traffic

(B) **Wholesale business,** a store front and depends on store front but does require warehouse capability and a front office.

A.   Retail Business

If your idea is for a retail business of some kind you have probably given it a lot of thought and you have either seen or have some experience in the kind of store you want. Perhaps you have even drawn pictures of how you envision the floor plan and exterior to be. That's good because you need those thoughts, but on the practical side of getting started you need to start planning and prepare to spend some money.

1. Is your concept sound, and have you done any market research to see if there is a need for your kind of store? Retail stores generally serve a given area, so we suggest that you do a personal survey, with clipboard in hand and some survey sheets that ask people or businesses if they will buy your product. Remember, you are not selling at this time, you

are gathering market information. Sound difficult? Hate the idea of going out and cold calling? Just remember, your success or failure depends on how you interact with customers, and if this is something you cannot do–then perhaps you need to re-think going into business.

2. Once you have this information go to your local library business reference desk and get the names of Retail Trade Associations that serve the interests of your kind of business. Contact them to find out what information they have and think about joining one of them. This can be a valuable resource for you. You will find demographic and important sales ratio information that will help later on as you plan for location and inventory.

3. Location is everything for a retail business. You cannot be successful if you try to get second best or save money here, just as it is a bad idea to select a very expensive location. Select your location carefully according to the needs of your market, and you may want to hire a location expert to find and negotiate the perfect spot for your business. Real estate people are generally not the best to choose because they will want to show you only the properties on which they get commissions. An independent location expert will consider the nature of your business; the demographics; traffic count and available properties in an area good for you.

4. Signs and store build-out are also important because it is part of your image. We recommend that sign requirements be done by sign companies because of zoning and licensing requirements. Advice from your Trade Association and even vendors is valuable in determining store lay-out. Take your time in making floor plans; visit similar stores in other cities. Ask the owners for their advice.

5. Contact your suppliers. You need to do this well in advance of signing the lease for your location. Be sure to have in writing their terms, minimum orders, shipping schedules, etc. They will generally work with you and help you get ready to open.

6. Check with your County Court House or Business License Office about required licenses and permits for your business. They may have a packet of information already made up that explains all this. They will need to know if you are a corporation or a proprietorship. Contact a business attorney to take care of this for you.

7. Contact a general insurance agent to get your business insurance. Do not open your doors unless you have liability coverage.

8. As you can see there are some expenses to incur before you ever open the doors. Our suggestion is that you write out a business plan right now. In it you need to list all of these expenses and to project expenses for your first two years. You can find a business plan description and outline in Appendix B of this manual. You can also find excellent

business plan information on www.sba.gov. If you think that you are going to need financing before you get started, the business plan will become part of your financial package. We suggest that you contact the SBA desk of your bank and discuss these requirements with them.

9. Assuming that you have read the above 8 items in starting a retail business, and now know what is involved, you may want to find out if there is a franchise program that will offer you the same challenge and the same retail experience you are anticipating.

B.   Wholesale Business

A wholesale business by our definition is one which involves sales only to retail businesses or to processors, and whose sales are largely sales tax exempt. No sales are made to individuals or to the general public. If this describes the business idea you have, then please proceed.

Those who start wholesale businesses generally have prior experience either in the buying or selling end of the wholesale product. Our experience has shown that these people have already established contacts in their specialty and know both the customer they will serve and the suppliers they will buy from. In many cases, their suppliers are the manufacturers of the products they will sell wholesale.

1. The first considerations are your sources of supply. Because you are serving as the sales arm for your suppliers, it is important that you establish a solid partnership, or working agreement with them. Many times this will be a contract that ties you together.

2. Understanding costs and the subsequent pricing of the products you sell is the essential key to success in the wholesale business. Primarily because you are working with margins that are not as wide as those you sell to. But you are selling in quantity, which makes the difference. In practically every specialty field there are trade associations who have all kinds of information about pricing, marketing and inventory systems. Be sure to contact the Trade Association that serves your industry.

3. Marketing your products is generally done with a sales staff that is either paid by commission salary or both. This is an area that requires a uniform policy. All sales or commission people must be treated equally and must sign non-compete agreements.

IV.   **E-Commerce**–Business done on the Internet.
        Bill Gates said, "The successful companies of the next decade will be the ones that use digital tools to reinvent the way they work." The term "electronic commerce" (e-Commerce) has evolved from meaning electronic shopping to representing all aspects of business and market processes enabled by the Internet. Any transaction over the

Internet involving the transfer of goods, services or information is considered e-Commerce.

E-Commerce is the total business process. When you are engaged in e-Commerce you will be applying today's technologies to streamline and enhance business interactions. This means radically different method for marketing, selling and delivering goods and services. The Internet will enable you to directly interface with any customer regardless of time or location, potentially eliminating face to face and telephone-based interactions.

Technology may be driving e-Commerce, but success in business is not about e-Commerce. It is about using technology to empower yourself, your business and your customers. No matter how high-tech you get, basic business tenets do not change. It is still about customers and sound business management. Developing a winning e-Commerce strategy requires a willingness to embrace change without abandoning sound management practices and great customer service.

1. Due Diligence—Learn as much as possible about e-Commerce opportunities in your industry. Building an e-strategy is more than just building a web-site and an e-mail address. It means establishing a business approach and a plan that outlines specific action steps that electronically integrate all components of your business.

    A. Use all available search engines to research topics related to your business. (See Appendix
    A. for a list of Business resource web addresses).
    B. Check with trade associations in your industry for information
    C. Attend seminars
    D. Visit your competition on the Web.

1. **Create a Vision**—Define where you want to go. Identify how e-Commerce will add a new dimension to your business. Establish your vision as a living part of your company. Keep your focus and stay committed to getting there.

2. **Build a Dynamic Business Plan**—This is a blueprint for growing and managing your business. See Chapter 10..

3. **Anticipate Change and Don't Go it Alone**—Look ahead for new opportunities. With the velocity of business increasing at a dramatic pace, true competitors will need to stay ahead or be lost in the shuffle. Strategic alliances are important to your business growth and survival. As a virtual integration becomes mainstream, businesses are recognizing

that continued success must be leveraged and that the days of the independent company are over. Develop partnerships for strength.

4. **Know Your Customers**–Talk and listen to your customers. Ask them what on-line products or services they want from your business. Initiate and read customer correspondence and surveys. Learn why your customers buy from you and why they don't. Knowing who your customers are and what they want is critical to your success. See Chapter 7.

5. **Embrace the Internet**–The Internet is the most powerful change agent in the new digital economy. Explore ways to exploit its connectivity to breakdown traditional barriers. Use the Internet to connect more directly to your customers, vendors, and partners. Learn from your competitors and explore opportunities that work for others

6. **Develop a Higher level of Customer Service**–Use the Internet to make it easier for customers to interact with your business. Streamline customer interactions and make it easier to buy products, and to get information. For example, use E-Bay, Amazon and any other successful internet marketing site to your advantage.

Creating a Web Site:

There are two primary ways you can accommodate Internet-based commerce. Someone can either build a web site and equip it for commerce or you can get an intermediary to host it for you. Keep one thing in mind, just because you have a web site does not mean customers will come to your site. There are literally thousands of web sites out there on every conceivable subject. You are like a needle in a hay stack. It needs to be marketed like any other business, and there are experts on the web who can do this kind of marketing for you. For small businesses with limited budgets I recommend www.sutherdyne.com as an excellent web design source

A well designed web site should have the following qualities:

1. Visually attractive and appealing. Have a graphic artist or web designer do this for you.
2. Simple to understand and navigate; people understand simple.
3. Shopping cart capabilities that are easy for customers to use.
4. Ordering must be automated.
5. Offers payment functions: Pay-Pal can set-up a charge card program for you.
6. Tracks customers.

There are many companies currently available who offer "e-Commerce solutions." These companies can be found on the Web or you may locate one in your area through the yellow pages or word of mouth. If this is of interest to you, talk to them about a turn-key program where they will build your web pages, maintain it and do the marketing by getting you on as many search engines as possible.

Do your homework. Become knowledgeable about your options by understanding what is available and what your needs really are. Knowledge, remember, is your most important asset in the new economy.

Appendix A

Website Address Directory

Updated November 2005 **SEARCH ENGINES**

AltaVista-www.altavista.com/
Dogpile-www.dogpile.com
Excite-www.excite.com/
Infoseek-www.infoseek.com
Lycos-www.lycos.com

Metacrawler-www.metacrawler.com
SEACH.com-www.search.com
Webcrawler-www.webcrawler.com/
Yahoo-www.yahoo.com/
Hot Bot-www.hotbot.com/ put exact words to limit search
Google–www.google.com. Best site to use

Business Owner's Resources/ Services/ Info

American Express: www.americanexpress.com/smallbiz
Biz@dvantage-www.biz.n2k.com-financial & credit data from Dunn & Bradstreet & other sources
BizProWeb-www.bizproweb.com resources & links to shareware business software
Biz Resource-www.bizresource.com
Business Owner's Toolkit: www.toolkit.cch.com
Digital Work-one stop small bus. services-www.digitalwork.com
Entrepreneurial Edge-"Business Toolbox" section helpful www.edgeonline.com
Idea Cafe-a fun approach to serious business: www.ideacafe.com-
Microsoft Small Business Website-www.microsoft.com/smallbiz
Mining Company, The-www.miningco.com
MoreBusiness.com-sample business & marketing plans, sample contracts: www.morebusiness.com
National Federation of Independent Businesses (NFIB): www.nfibonline.com

National Assoc. of the Self-Employed (NASE): www.nase.org
National Business Incubation Assoc.: www.nbia.org
Netscape Small Business Info-www.netscape.com
Quicken-www.quicken.com/small business
SCORE (Service Corp of Retired Executives): www.score.org
Self Help Credit Union: www.selfhelp.org
Small Business Administration: www.sbaonline.sba.gov/
Smartbiz-thousands of Free how-to resources-www. srnartbiz.com
Visa USA-www.visa.com/smallbiz

Business Plans

Quicken-www.quicken.com/small business
Palo Alto Software, free samples and links: www.bplans.com (the best)
BestBizplan.com-fee based: www.bestbizplan.com

Buying/ Selling A Business

Empire Business Brokers: www.empirebusinessbrokers.com Search engine for buyers: www.bizbuysell.com Selling A Business by MetLife: www.metlife.com/Lifeadvice VR Business Brokers: www.vrbusinessbrokers.com

Demographics

American Demographics magazine: www.marketingtools.com
Census: www.census.gov/stat-abstract
Easi Demographics: www.easidemographics.com
Federal Interagency Council-statistics provided by federal agencies: www.Fedstats.gov
State of NC demographics: www.ospl.state.nc.us/demog

Discussion Groups/ Search Engines

Dejanews www.dejanews.com
Let's Talk Business Network-www.ltbn.com
Inter-Links: good links www.alabanza.com/kabacoff/Inter-Links

Electronic Commerce

AAA Internet Promotions-promotes websites: http://netmar.com

Bizserve from Online Technologies: www.bizserve.com

CommerceNet-industry association of organizations doing business on the internetzzz; www.commerce.net

Idealab-resources for starting a business on the internet-www.idealab.com

Interpath Communications-turnkey ebusiness solutions: www.ncsmallbiz.com

Worldwide Entrepreneur World-resources for using the web: www.worldentre.com

Yoursource-website design, hosting, marketing: www.voursource.com

Employee Info

Employee Benefits Research Institute: www.ebri.org

Employment Laws-interactive advice & info on the latest regulatory laws: www.dol.gov/elaws

Equal Employment Opportuity, Office of: www. gsa. gov/eeo

JobSmart Profession Specific Salary survey   www.jobsmart.org/tools/salary/sal-prof.htm

National Employee Benefits-www.benefitslmk.com

Family Business

Arthur Andersen Center for Family Business: www.arthurandersen.com/cfb

Families & Work Institute (NYC): www.familiesandwork.org

Family Business Network-hit'l Institute for Management Dev.-enter Family in search: www.imd.ch

The Family Firm Institute membership listing: www.ffi.org

Federal Agencies

Census Department-www.census.gov

Consmer Information Center-www.pueblo.gsa.gov

Environmental Protection Agency: www.epa.gov

Federal Trade Commission-www.ftc.gov

International Trade Admin.: www.ita.doc.gov

National Climatic Data Center: www.ncdc.noaa.gov

Occupational Safety & Health Admin.(OSHA): www.osha.gov

Small Business Administration: www. sbaonline. sba. gov/

Small Business Regulatory Board: www.sbaonline.sba.gov/regfair

Women's Business support programs: www.sbaonline.sba.gov/womeninbusiness

US Dept. of Commerce: www.doc.gov

US Government Online Gateway: www.fedworld.gov

White House Conference on Small Business-dated, but links section is good: www.whcsb.org

Financial/ Stock Market

Bloomberg Business News-www.bloomberg.com

Corporate Financials Online-financials on mostly smaller companies: www.cfonews.com

Daily Market Reports-www.stockgroup.com

Quote.Com-www.quote.com

NETworth-mutual fund data www.quicken.com/investinents

New York Stock Exchange: www.nyse.com

Stock Market Guide-www.onlineinvestors.com

StockMaster-www. stockmaster. com

Financing/ Loans

Access to Captial Electronic Network (Ace-Net)-search secure database for venture cap.: www.ace-net.org

American Express Small Business Exchange-www.americanexpress.com/smallbusiness

Bank of America-www.bofa.com/business/home.html

BusinessFinance.com-www.businessfinance.com free search enginefor all forms of funds

Capital.com: www.capital.com

Datamerge-(sourcing capital)-www.datamerge.com

FinanceHub-www.financehub.com

First Union & The Money Store-www.firstunion.com/smallbusiness

Forbes Small Business Center-www.forbes.com/growing

LiveCapital.com-comparison shop for financing: www.LiveCapital.com

Money-www.money.com

MoneyHunter-www.monevhunter.com

Onlineinvestors.com: www.onlineinvestors.com

PrimeStreet.com: www.PrimeStreet.com

Quicken Small Business-www.quicken.com/smallbusiness

Self Help Credit Union: www.self-help.org

Small Business Administration-www.sba.gov

Small Business Development Center-www.businessfinance.com/sbdc.asp

Small Business Innovation Research Program(SBIR)-www.acq.osd.mil/sadbu/sbir
US Investor Network: www.usinvestor.com
Visa USA-www.visa.com/smallbiz
Wells Fargo-the nation's #1 small business lender www.biz.wellsfargo.com

Franchises

American Assoc. of Franchise and Dealers: www.aafd.org
Continental Franchise Review: www.cfrnews.com
Franchise UPDATE publication: www.Franchise-Update.com
Francorp, Inc.: www.francorpinc.com
Global info for franchises: www.franchise-conxions.com
International Franchise Assoc.: www.franchise.org
Info about individual franchises: www.franchisesolutions.com

Home-based Businesses

Business@Home-info, on starting a home-based bus-www.gohome.com Working Solo
free newsletter: www.workingsolo.com

Incorporating

Corporate Agents: www.corporate.com
EDGAR-Sec filings of US companies-www.edgar-online.com
Nolo Selp-Help Law Center-www.nolo.com

IRS/ Taxes

Deloitte & Touche Tax News (1997 tax law): www.dtonline.com/promises/chap8.htm
IRS Tax Forms & Publications-www.irs.usfreas.gov
Kiplinger TaxCut-www.taxcut.com
Nolo Self-Help Law Center-www.nolo.com
Qualified Business Investment Tax Credit Program:
www.secstate.state.nc.us/secstate/tax.htm
Small Business Taxes & Management (online magazine): www.smbiz.com
TaxSites-www.taxsites.com
TurboTax-www.webturbotax.com
Universal Tax Systems-www. securetax.com
NC Institute of Minority Economic Development e-mail address: ncimed@nando.net

NC Office of State Planning: www.ospl.state.nc.us
NC Secretary of State: www.state.nc.us/secstate/
NC State Telephone Directory: www.state.nc.us/phone

Patent/Trademark Information

Biz@dvantage-www.biz.n2k.com IBM Patent Server: www.ibm.com/patents Oppedahl &
Larson law firm-www.patents. com Patent Search System: www.sunsite.unc.edu/patents
Product Testing: www.product-testing.com SB A-www.sba.gov/tibrary/pubs/pi-3.txt US
Patent & Trademark Office: www.uspto.gov
Virtual Library Law Intellectual Property-maintained by Indiana Univ. School of Law:
www.law.indiana.edu/law/v-lib/intellect

Publications/ Communication

Magazines/ News/ Newspapers
Advertising News: www.adage.com
American Demographics Magazine: www.marketingtools.com
Bloomberg-www.bloomberg.com/sniallbiz
Business Wire: www.businesswire.com
CNN interactive: www.cnn.com.
ClariNet-news from Reuters, UPI: www.ClariNet.com
Drudge Report (headlines of all major print media): www.Drudgereport.com
Entrepreneur Magazine: www.entrepreneurmag.CQm

Inc. Magazine: www.inc.com
Infomanage-international trade resources and links: www.infomanage.coni
Media News: www.mediacentral.com
NC Entrepreneur Magazine: www.ncentrepreneur.com
Nando Times: www.nando.net/nt/biz
New York Times: www.nytimes.com
News & Observer: www.news-observer.com
Pathfinder-massive Time-Warner site: www.pathfinder.com
Science Magazine: www. sciencemag.org
Selling Power: www.sellingpower.com
The Small Business Journal: www.tsbi.com
USA Today latest news edition: www.usatodav.com

Wall Street Journal:www.wsj.com Newsletters
Communication Briefings: www.combriefings.com
Working Solo: www.workingsolo.com
The Marketing Minute-free service: major domo@world.std.com type message
"subscribe marketii Books
Deloitte & Touche Tax News www.dtonline.com/promise/chap8.htni
Guerrilla Marketing-Jay Conrad www. gmarketing.com
Library of Congress Catalog-can locate obscure books and other text-
www.loc.gov Phone Directories
AT&T Services: www.att.com
Big Book-includes customer reviews of businesses: www.bigbook.com
Canada Yellow Pages: www.canadayellowpages.com
Family & Business Directory: www.fbdi.com
Fourll: www.fourl 1.com
National Direct Internet Yellow Pages: www.ndiyp.com
Site Promoter-list your site with 150 search engines for $97: www. sitepromoter.com
Switchboard: www.switchboard.com
Yellow Pages: www.yellowpage.net

Selling to the Government

Acquisition Reform Network-govn't procurement regulations & requirements:
www.arnet.gov
Clarinet News: www.ClariNet.com/cbd general.html
Electronic Commerce Resource Center: www.ecrc.ctc.com/index.htrn
www.fedmarket.com-how to sell to Uncle Sam
Small Business Administration (SBA)-www.sbaonline.sba.gov/expanding
SBA's government contracting Web page-www.sba.gov/gc
SBA's Web page for PRO-Net-www.pro-net. sba. gov
Summary of bids from Dept of Defense-www.acq.osd.mil/ec
Source for *Commerce Business Daily*: www.fcw.com/ref/cbd.htm
US Business Advisor's Web page: www.business. gov
U.S. General Service Administration's primer: www.gsa.gov
Daily issue: www.ld.com/cbd/today/index.html-ssi

US Government Purchasing & Sales Directory: www.access.gpo/su docs
USPS details & regulations: www.usps.gov

Small Business Training/Courses/Seminars

Good Works-non-profit-www. goodwork.org
NC Real Entrepreneurship-non-profit thru Community Colleges & high schools-www.ncreeal.org
Central Piedmont Community College-www.cpcc.edu (click on Continuing Education)

Suppliers & Wholesalers for Small Business

Thomas Register-identify suppliers and competitors:
www.thomasregister.com/index www.ecomall. com/business/menu.htm

Surveys

Survey Pro: www.apian.com
SurveySolutions: www.perseusdevlopment.com
Survey Systems: www.survevsvstem.com
Insight Research, Inc (fee-based): www.insightresearchinc.com

Trade Shows/ Conferences

CyberEXPO: www.cvberexpo.com
EventSource: www.eventsource.com
ExpoBase: www.expo base.com
Expoguide: www.expoguide.com
Expoweb-official site for Expo magazine: www.expoweb.com
IMEX Exchange: www.assist-intl.com
Trade Show Central: www.tscentral.com
Trade Show News Network: www.tsnn.com
TradeShow Week: www.tradeshoweek.com

Website Design/ Hosts

www.sutherdyne.com–best for small start-up businesses
Cyber Submit-www.cvbersubmit.com
Franklin Pierce Law Center feature on "Copyright on the Internet"-
www.internetlegal.com/article.htrn
Inside the Web—add a message board to site: www.InsideTheWeb.com
The Ultimate Web Host List-www.webhostlist.com

Web Law FAQ-www.patents.com/weblaw.sht
Wilson Internet Services-web marketing & e-commerce: www.wilsonweb.com

Women

Free networking: www.BizWomen.com
Home-based Working Moms (TX) free membership: www.hbwm.com
National Association of Women Business Owners-www.nawbo.org
National Foundation for Women Business Owners-www.nfwbo.org/
National Women's Business Council-www.womenconnect.com/

Online Women's Business Center-www.onlinewbc.org
SBA support programs for women in business:
www.sbaonline.sba.gov/womeninbusiness
Women's Resource Directory: www.ghgcorp.com/wordweb

Miscellaneous

Books about American consumers-www.newstrategist.com
CitySearch: www.citysearch11.com
City Net: www.city.net
Daycare info.-www.webcom.com/seaquest/sbrc/daycare
How to find a lawyer for your bus-American Bar Association-www.abanet.org or
www.lawyers.com
National Mail Order Association-features products in newsletter to wholesale buyers-
www.nmoa.org
National Fraud Information Center-www.fraud.org
Quotesmith.com-free insurance quotes online-www.quotesmith.com
Scams-Better Business Bureau: www.bbb.org
US Postal Service Zip Code Info.: www.uspo.gov
www.liszt.com-join an email list, newsgroup, or business newsletter

Index of Subjects

Index of Subjects

References

1. Advocacy Office of the Small Business Administration, *Small Business Research*. www.SBA.gov/advo

2. Research Department, American Express. www.AmericanExpress.com

3. Hatten, Timothy, *Small Business, Entrepreneurship and Beyond,* Prentice Hall, 1997, p 24.

4. Timmons, J. and Spinelli, S., *New Venture Creation,* Sixth Edition. McGraw Hill-Irwin, New York, 2004, p 79.

5. Bizminer 2002 Industry Statistics, www.bizminer.com

6. *Ibid.* SBA Advocacy Office.

7. *Ibid.* Timmons and Spinelli, p 15.

8. Carland, JW. *Portraits of Potential Entrepreneurs,* Journal of Business and Entrepreneurship. (5)1, March 1993, pp 59-66.

9. *Ibid,* SBA Advocacy Office.

10. Metcalf, William, *Starting and Managing Your Own Small Business*, Vol. 1 SBA Office of Business Development, 1958, U.S. Superintendent of Documents.

11. Ray, M. and Myers, M., *Creativity in Business*, Doubleday, 1989, pp 77

978-0-595-40037-9
0-595-40037-X

Printed in the United States
66336LVS00004B/18

9 780595 400379